RELATIONSHIP HARMONY HACKS

RELATIONSHIP HARMONY HACKS

Crack the Code of Male and Female Instincts for Vibrant, Respectful, and Peaceful Partnerships

BARBARA COLE SALMERON

Published by Best Seller Publishing®, St. Augustine, FL
Best Seller Publishing® is a registered trademark.
Printed in the United States of America.

ISBN: 9781962595490

For more information, please write:
Best Seller Publishing®
1775 US-1 #1070
St. Augustine, FL 32084
or call 1 (626) 765-9750

Visit us online at: www.BestSellerPublishing.org

Table of Contents

This book is dedicated to three wonderful men who have shown the world how to be loving fathers and husbands: My late dad, Travis Cole, my husband's late dad, John Salmeron, and especially my husband, Rick Salmeron, whose unyielding love and support made this book, and so much more, possible! I love you, honey; you'll always be my favorite person!

Introduction

> **You can't connect the dots looking forward; you can only connect them looking backward.**
>
> **So, you have to trust that the dots will somehow connect in your future.**
>
> STEVE JOBS

Have you ever been confused, mystified, or downright bewildered by the opposite sex? I know I have! Before I learned how to *connect the dots* between human instinct and behavior, I was an absolute HOT MESS in my romantic relationships with men. I was forty years old and going through yet another breakup. I *knew* that it was my last chance to have children. I was exhausted and felt very hopeless in my quest to find my person. For over a decade, I'd had a series of short, failed, painful relationships that lasted just three to four months. After that, I'd decide that the guy just wasn't right for me and initiate the breakup. Again and again, the men were usually blindsided because they didn't even know there was anything wrong! I was not good at asking for what I needed; I didn't even know what my own needs were back then.

I saw a definite pattern emerge. I was consistently becoming the *masculine* or else the *mommy* in my relationships with men, and I didn't want to be either of those things in my romantic life. So, back in 2014, after a decade of this, I knew I needed to do something different. Thanks to years of personal and spiritual growth work, I was able to recognize that I was the common denominator here. I was somehow creating this result over and over again. All the men I dated were great guys because I don't date jerks! So, somehow, I was unwittingly bringing out the worst in them instead of the best. At the time of this realization, my then-boyfriend and I were fighting every single day. I felt the end was near, and I was completely exhausted and depleted from severe adrenal fatigue (more on that later!). I had just turned forty, and I knew that the possibility of having children was quickly slipping away. It was right at that time that I met my mentor, Alison Armstrong.

I was living in Hawaii and was set to attend her first-ever workshop there, called Understanding Men. The first morning, as I was leaving for the workshop, my boyfriend and I had another big fight. On my way to the workshop, I was distraught, crying, and so angry and frustrated over the past several weeks of daily fighting. Thankfully, a friend was with me, and she was able to coach me back to a state of calm using the Emotional Freedom Technique (EFT), also known as *tapping*. I clearly remember that the very first part of the Understanding Men workshop was so impactful that on the first break, I called my boyfriend, in tears, to apologize. Just in that first segment, I began to see how very different men *truly* are from women and that *my* assumptions and misunderstandings about men had caused most of the trouble all along.

I continued to study with Alison, and while my relationship with my then-boyfriend ultimately ended, my very next one did not! I moved to Dallas, Texas, in 2015 and met my true love. My very next relationship, after learning about men, was with my now-husband, Rick. We married in 2018 and have the best relationship either of us has ever experienced. He feels respected and appreciated, and I feel loved and cherished as we've developed a true partnership together, full of intimacy and trust. I want everyone to experience this level of love, respect, and security! With Rick's encouragement and support, I became certified and licensed by Alison in sixteen different topics to share in whatever way I like. As a PAX-Certified Partner (PAX is the name of her company; it means peace in Latin), I am committed to getting this illuminating and groundbreaking material out into the world so that more people can experience relationship harmony in their own lives.

I've created sixteen masterclasses (available at www.Grow.BarbaraColeSalmeron.com) and now this book. I use this incredible, life-changing material in my coaching, my speaking engagements, my writing, and in podcast, TV, and radio interviews. My goal is to share these concepts with as many humans as possible because this work applies to *much more than just heterosexual romantic relationships!* Because these teachings are based on human instinct and the differences between the male and female brain, you will find them invaluable in your family and work relationships. You will better understand your friends too! Please help me spread the word so I can help others experience love, peace, respect, and intimacy in their relationships. When we truly understand the opposite sex, we can turn our relationship conflict into deeply loving partnerships at home, at work, and in romance!

> **Throughout this book I have included quotes from my research interviews.**
> **The names of the people interviewed have been changed in order to respect their privacy and maintain confidentiality.**

Note: This material is based on over three decades of research interviews with men and women. Most of the people interviewed were in North America, the United Kingdom, and Europe and identified as the gender determined at birth. If you identify differently, this work is also for you because we're mostly discussing human instinct! In fact, if you identify as nonbinary, gender-fluid, transgender, two-spirit, intersex, another gender, or LGBTQIA+, *I want to interview you!* Please email me at Love@BarbaraColeSalmeron.com with the subject line *Research Interview*. I am an ally, and my heart hurts for your pain of being born into a fearful world that lacks understanding and acceptance. No matter your gender, age, or sexual orientation, the research and tools I share in this book and in my masterclasses will help you in your relationships with other humans!

It is normal and natural that we all see the world from our unique point of view. For example, if you happen to love chocolate, you might tend to think that others love chocolate, too. Our own levels of integrity, work ethic, and so on are also often assumed and projected as truth onto others. Our worldview is based on our lifetime experiences, so it's easy to assume others will (or should!) think and behave the way we do. However, this is absolutely not true, especially when it comes to the opposite

> **Our worldview is based on our lifetime experiences, so it's easy to assume others will (or should!) think and behave the way we do.**
>
> **However, this is absolutely not true, especially when it comes to the opposite sex!**
>
> BARBARA COLE SALMERON

sex! These invisible expectations cause so many misunderstand-ings in our relationships with other people.

**Are you ready to consider a new point of view
with regard to the battle of the sexes?**

**Are you ready to take the boxing gloves
off to create loving partnerships?**

**Are you ready to experience the best
in your relationships?**

I truly hope so; let's go!

Disclaimer: This material will *not* be *applicable* to those who find joy in abusing or harming others. Physical, mental, financial, and emotional abuse are *never* accept-able! People who are incapable of feeling love or remorse, such as extreme narcissists, psychopaths, or sociopaths, are master manipulators when it comes to lying, deceiv-ing, gaslighting, and so on. Those with such personality disorders make up a very small percentage of the popu-lation, but they can be very dangerous. If you suspect any form of abuse in your relationship, I urge you to educate yourself on the *incurable personality disorders* listed above and *get help* in creating safety for yourself.

But First ... It's All About Testosterone!

Testosterone Is the Fuel

Men have always had an innate instinct to protect and provide, and testosterone is their fuel for getting things done. It just keeps them going. It keeps them focused on the job and supports them in producing results and providing for the family. Men have ten to thirty-two times more testosterone than women do, and that is very significant!

According to Dr. Louann Brizendine, in her books *The Male Brain* and *The Female Brain*, all babies first start developing with a female brain. This changes (or doesn't) at about eight weeks after conception, depending on whether the fertilizing sperm brought the X or Y chromosome to the party![1,2] In *The Female Brain*, Dr. Brizendine says the following:

---

[1] Louann Brizendine, M.D., *The Male Brain: A Breakthrough Understanding of How Men and Boys Think,* January 1, 2011. Three Rivers Press

[2] Louann Brizendine, M.D., *The Female Brain,* August 7, 2007. Harmony

Until eight weeks old, every fetal brain looks female — female is nature's default gender setting ... A huge testosterone surge beginning in the eighth week will turn the unisex brain male by killing off some cells in the communication centers and growing more cells in the sex and aggression centers. If the testosterone surge doesn't happen, the female brain continues to grow unperturbed. The fetal girl's brain cells sprout more connections in the communication centers and areas that process emotion. How does this fetal fork in the road affect us? For one thing, because of her larger communication center, this girl will grow up to be more talkative than her brother. Men use about seven thousand words per day. Women use about twenty thousand. For another, it defines our innate biological destiny, coloring the lens through which each of us views and engages with the world.

I *highly* recommend reading or listening to Dr. Brizendine's books, especially if you are a parent! To recap: After conception, the developing brain of the baby is female, by default, until about eight weeks, and *if* a flood of testosterone happens, the brain becomes male. After that, the developing male baby brain has *fewer* cells in the communication centers and *more* cells in the aggression and sex centers! The developing female brain grows *more connections* in the areas of communication and emotion. Are you starting to see how very different men and women are *before we are even born?* Why, then, do we expect the opposite sex to behave like us, think like us, or feel like us (and vice versa)? We *must* accept the realities of the differences between the sexes if we are ever to come into harmony with each other! Learning about these innate, instinctual differences between the sexes, as well as effective communication skills, is what *this* book is about.

Now that you know some of the science that my work is based on, I want to share some key things about men and women for you to keep in mind as you explore our magnificent differences. Let's start with the *superpowers* for the male and female brains. Men have a superpower we call Single Focus, and this is due to the difference in brain structure between the sexes, and because of their much higher testosterone levels. The male brain is more likely to focus on a single task at a time and needs to have transition time to shift over to a different task. The amount of transition time needed depends on the intensity of the tasks he is shifting from and to. If you would like to learn more about transition time and transition rituals, I've prepared a bonus chapter for you online, which can be found at BarbaraColeSalmeron.com/Books.

> **Men have a superpower we call Single Focus, and this is due to the difference in brain structure between the sexes, and because of their much higher testosterone levels.**
>
> BARBARA COLE SALMERON

While women don't usually achieve Single Focus (due to our higher estrogen levels), we can have a very high level of focus when we are in Hunting Mode, which we will discuss in Chapter 2. Women have a superpower we'll call Diffuse Awareness. *To diffuse* means to pour in every direction. Because of our Diffuse Awareness, we *notice everything*. We see all the details in our environment, such as the pillow that needs to be straightened and the floor that still needs to be mopped. We remember the email we forgot to answer and the phone call we need to make today. We think about our doctor's appointment that we have tomorrow morning, and we wonder whether we've already told our boss we will be late tomorrow. We notice everything around us, and those things are each *calling out to us,* pulling us in every direction and *screaming* for our attention. It's no wonder women feel overwhelmed so frequently in their day-to-day lives! Can you relate?

It doesn't stop there! We also feel and notice the emotional, mental, and physical state of everyone and everything in our environment. We can tell when our honey is upset, and we can even tell when our pet isn't feeling well. We also believe that this is where multitasking comes from, which we will explore further in Chapter 2.

Men definitely have an edge in that testosterone is an advantage for focus and producing results. Burnout and adrenal fatigue are on the rise for women, in large part because we do not have the testosterone reserves that men do, yet we're working full-time jobs, just like men, and coming home to our families (another full-time job!). This is exactly how I damaged my health. I was actually working three jobs at a time, an example I saw modeled by both of my parents, and I ended up with severe adrenal fatigue.

I've created another bonus chapter for you that goes into adrenal fatigue and several other topics about women's health that are usually missed or misdiagnosed by Western medicine doctors. The other topics in the bonus chapter include bioidentical hormones (especially testosterone), being undiagnosed neurodivergent, adrenal fatigue, burnout, and the cure for alcoholism. You read that right ... there *is* a cure for alcoholism that does not require abstinence, has a 78 percent success rate, and has

been studied by an American doctor in over four decades of medical research. It's called the Sinclair Method, or TSM. I am *so passionate* that women *know* about these topics because they took me a lifetime of difficulty to discover, and the vast majority of Western medicine doctors *won't educate themselves* on these solutions, much less their patients. Please grab a copy of my free bonus chapter at BarbaraColeSalmeron.com/Books and share it with every woman you know!

One

Human Normal and Human Spirit

> **If you change the way you look at things, the things you look at change.**
>
> DR. WAYNE DYER

There is an aspect of human duality that we (my mentor, colleagues, and I) call Human Normal and Human Spirit. Human Normal is that part of us that operates on instinct, while Human Spirit allows us to respond from a place of choice, patience, and compassion. Let's start with Human Normal by first understanding the word *instinct*.

The Britannica Dictionary defines "instinct" as follows:

a)   *1 a: a way of behaving, thinking, or feeling that is not learned: a natural desire or tendency that makes you want to act in a particular way*

b)   *b: something you know without learning it or thinking about it.*

In this context, we relate to instinct as a primal, biological urge compelling us to seek relief from tension. *Primal,* meaning "first," tells us that this is biological, and it's *not* something that can be fixed by therapy! A primal, biological urge revolves around the basic needs of food, shelter, and safety or protection. To be compelled means that we are *overpowered* by a forceful or irresistible influence. The tension rising in our bodies is a great indication that one of our survival instincts is being triggered. We are compelled to have a knee-jerk reaction to relieve that discomfort quickly. That is exactly what happens when we automatically react by saying or doing something that we usually regret later.

Even in our modern-day lives, if our brain thinks our survival is somehow threatened, our Human Normal instincts can appear without notice, and we can experience an internal cavewoman or caveman attack, which is how I refer to having a meltdown triggered by our Human Normal instincts. We *must* find compassion for ourselves and see the humor in these situations because we are all human, after all! I will repeatedly remind you that *you are not a bad person* if you see evidence of

> **Instinct: A primal, biological urge, compelling us to seek relief from tension.**
>
> BARBARA COLE SALMERON

these very normal reactions in your own life. I do believe we are all doing the best we can with where we are, as said by the late, great Maya Angelou.

Forgive yourself for past mistakes; otherwise, they will control your future. You will be learning so many new things in this book, which will help you to consciously shape your relationships for the better, moving forward. So, go easy on yourself throughout this journey! Because no matter how enlightened we become, we still have needs, and the Human Normal instincts are so well ingrained in an effort to keep us alive. In fact, your brain sees its number one job as keeping you alive, *not* happy! Your brain doesn't care whether you are happy as long as your heart is beating, your lungs are functioning, and so on. Knowing this, it's no wonder that almost everyone can relate to falling short in their relationships.

> **Do the best you can until you know better. Then when you know better, do better.**
>
> MAYA ANGELOU

I can just hear my most spiritual friends claiming their immunity from Human Normal, yet alas, we *all* require food, shelter, and protection. And while I don't claim to have reached enlightenment, I began my journey of personal and spiritual growth in 1999 as a seeker of a deeper understanding of how life works. I've studied topics that range from shamanism to psychology, and I consider myself a lifelong learner. I've learned what makes humans tick, and yet I *still* have these basic needs for the sake of survival, as does every human being I know. Our brain's neural pathways (how the brain is naturally wired) haven't changed very much in thousands of years, even though our survival looks quite different today than it did back then! Today, we don't have to live in cold caves or hunt for our food; we can just hunt and gather from the wide variety of delicious products at the grocery store and bring them home with ease. We don't need to build a fire to cook our food; we can just put it on the stovetop or in the Crock-Pot or Instant Pot, and voilà, we can savor our meals almost instantaneously!

Life has become more comfortable in many ways, and yet these humorous survival instincts are still alive and well; we haven't outgrown them. What has changed is our modern-day interpretation of them. We no longer have tigers hiding in the grass; we have potential predators lurking online. We don't have to make our own clothing; however, watch out if someone folds the towels "wrong" and they don't fit in the cupboard! We don't need to keep our kitchen spotless to avoid attracting wild animals, yet if someone loads the dishwasher "wrong," then we might insist on doing it again, the "right" way. Notice especially the instincts around cleanliness and food. Today's non-life-threatening events trigger our survival instinct because, back in the day of the cave people, we had procedures that needed to be meticulously followed, especially around food. It was crucial that things got done in a particular order and in a certain way; otherwise, people could get sick or even die. Can you feel the connection?

When we suppress or deny the Human Normal side of us, it's like taking a giant beach ball and holding it a few feet underwater. It's going to take a lot of energy and exertion to do that! It's physically exhausting, and as soon as we're distracted, the ball is just going to pop right back up to the surface. So rather than wasting our precious energy suppressing or denying our Human Normal, we can instead harness the energy and potency of our instincts. We can then elevate them into a higher expression by consciously shifting into Human Spirit (more on that soon).

We can tell that one of our survival instincts has been activated when we notice ourselves holding our breath or tensing our shoulders. Someone is saying or doing something we don't like; we start to feel the tension rising in our bodies; we might be biting our tongue or feeling uncomfortable emotions like fear, anxiety, or anger beginning to grow. If we don't stop ourselves, we can experience an instant knee-jerk reaction, which happens *before* we even know it's happening. And by then, it's already happened! Sound familiar?

> When we suppress or deny the Human Normal side of us, it's like taking a giant beach ball and holding it a few feet underwater.
> It's going to take a lot of energy and exertion to do that!
>
> BARBARA COLE SALMERON

Our first goal is just to start recognizing when we feel triggered in any way. We want to remember that the physical and emotional tension is *telling us something*. The brain feels our survival is at stake, even when there is no actual danger present. So, we want to notice the discomfort growing, stop ourselves, and then *celebrate* that we noticed. When we actually celebrate our noticing, we tell our brain, "Listen up, this is important!" which helps us identify it more easily next time. We can then clean it up a little sooner, and eventually, we can stop having those outbursts quite as often or even catch ourselves *before* we have our Human Normal knee-jerk reaction.

Shifting into Human Spirit

The opposite of Human Normal is Human Spirit, which is more about the enhancement of life, such as through art, music, beauty, and philanthropy. We don't need these things for our survival, although I admit they sure do make life more pleasurable, enjoyable, and worth living! Human Spirit is also when we are at our best, and we can choose to respond rather than give in to an unconscious reaction. We have access to expressing generosity, patience, genuine curiosity, and compassion when coming from Human Spirit.

When we are able to shift, we celebrate and call it a *Victory of Human Spirit!* One way to make the shift happen is just to stop and take a few deep breaths. Other methods are counting to ten or pausing by taking a long drink of water. When a survival instinct is triggered, we'll likely feel some kind of tension in the body, which is our instinct saying either we are in danger or someone else is in danger. While taking several deep breaths to shift ourselves into Human Spirit, we can remind ourselves that no one's going to die if the dishwasher gets loaded "wrong." Nothing horrible will happen if the towels get folded "wrong." We can walk out of the room to prevent a reaction we may later regret. When I feel the tension rising, I just say "Thank you for helping me with that!" and walk out of the room because *no towel or dish or toilet seat is more valuable to me than my marriage!* When we can recognize that our instinct is making something feel more dire than it really is, we can choose happiness instead. We can choose peace. We can choose to *let it go!* Being right is actually another survival instinct because, in part, in ancient times, being wrong had serious consequences! If you've ever been in a relationship with someone who insists on always being right, you know how exhausting and invalidating that can be. It also causes so much damage to our relationships.

> **We have access to expressing generosity, patience, genuine curiosity, and compassion when coming from Human Spirit.**
>
> BARBARA COLE SALMERON

Human Spirit is all about empowerment versus manipulation. Manipulation is an expected reaction when we are in Human Normal because, at some level, our brain feels like our survival is at stake. When we were first born, we had to have someone take care of us, or we wouldn't have made it! By crying or fussing, we "manipulated" our parents or caregivers into feeding us or soothing us. When we learn what works with each caregiver, we tend to stick to that. Have you ever experienced a child asking for a cookie from one parent after the other one has already said no? And if both parents say no, the child can go sweet talk Grandma into giving them what they want. That sweet talk and batting of the eyelashes is manipulation! It's not always something evil; it is a *learned way* of getting our needs and wants fulfilled.

When one of our survival instincts is triggered, it's completely normal to fall into manipulation to get our needs met. However, if we can shift into Human Spirit, then we can focus on empowerment instead. We can empower ourselves and empower others with whom we want to be in a partnership. When we form partnerships with other people, whether it's in friendship, in marriage, or at work, we're in Human Spirit, and we can come from a place of empowerment because we

> **When we can recognize that our instinct is making something feel more dire than it really is, we can choose happiness instead. We can choose peace. We can choose to let it go!**
>
> BARBARA COLE SALMERON

> **You can be right, or you can be happy.**
>
> GERALD G. JAMPOLSKY, AUTHOR OF *LOVE IS LETTING GO OF FEAR*

care about having these relationships work. It is truly a win-win because when we are at our best, we can then bring out the best in others. Over the years, I've learned that the quality of my relationships is directly related to my ability to bring out the best or the worst in others. In the upcoming pages, I will share with you the tools that can transform your relationships. These exact concepts in my books and masterclasses are what taught me how I was bringing out the worst in others and how to bring out the best in them instead! These exact tools are how I went from a *hot mess to happily ever after* in my romantic relationships, and my hope is that I can shorten that confusing, painful road for you!

Shifting into Human Spirit allows us to experience understanding and compassion for the other person. We can also have a genuine curiosity about them when we hit the pause button before reacting. From a place of curiosity, we can ask ourselves two key questions, "What if there's a good reason for that?" and "What if nobody is misbehaving?" Curiosity and giving someone the benefit of the doubt *does not* live in Human Normal! Generosity and abundance also come from Human Spirit, while scarcity and black-and-white thinking come from Human Normal. I'm sure you can see areas in your life where you are naturally in Human Spirit and other areas where you struggle with it. Remember to forgive yourself and have compassion for yourself. Notice these concepts in yourself and others, celebrate the noticing, and then simply strive to do better moving forward ... You've got this!

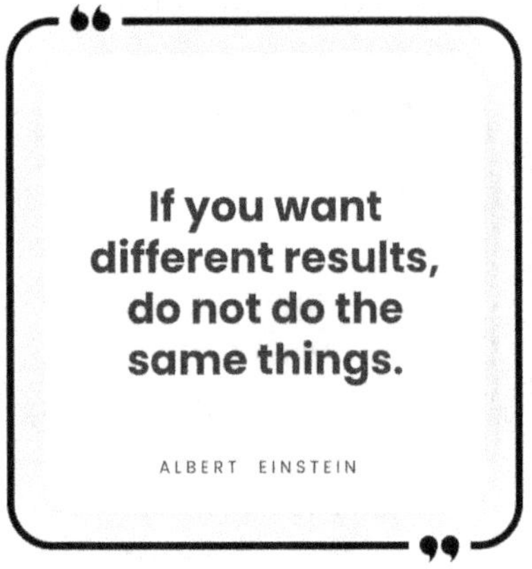

Elevate Our Choices

One example of how Human Normal and Human Spirit can work together is in the need for food. We all need food. I could choose to live on donuts and coffee or pizza and beer, and I would survive for years! It wouldn't be a very healthy existence; however, it would fulfill the survival instinct of needing food. Now, a conscious, elevated option in this example would be to make a different choice, such as eating paleo, vegetarian, or another healthy diet. By choosing an elevated expression, I will live a much different life. I'll be healthier, I'll be happier, and I'll probably live longer! If I want to have a healthy body bubbling with energy, I'll need to elevate my choices around food and not just let myself run on instinct, which will always look for the fastest, easiest, and most delicious dopamine-inducing choice!

Similarly, we can make an elevated choice in our relationships. The knee-jerk reaction comes from the brain's subconscious perception of danger. Our subconscious mind is very powerful and actually runs the show most of the time. Shifting into Human Spirit allows us to push the pause button on instinct and reactivity, access the conscious part of our brain, and make a different choice. Because, let's face it, am I really going to get the result I want if I criticize him *yet again?* I've asked him to pick up his socks how many times now? While I know firsthand how frustrating things like this can be in a relationship, I learned the hard way that how I was handling it was never going to get me the result I wanted. I had to be willing to *do* something completely *new,* and I truly hope you will be willing to do so as well.

> **If you want something you've never had, you must be willing to do something you've never done.**
>
> THOMAS JEFFERSON

Instinct versus Choice

If you are ready to do something new in order to experience a new outcome in your most important relationships, then I'm excited for the magic you are about to create in your life! Look at the lists below and ask yourself, "Which relationship would I want to be in?"

Which Relationship Would You Prefer?

Instinct	Choice
• Survival	• Elevated expression
• Reacting	• Responding
• Judgment	• Curiosity
• Scarcity	• Abundance
• One answer	• Many solutions
• Problems	• Possibilities
• Suspicion	• Benefit of the doubt
• Fear	• Love
• Manipulation	• Partnership
• Criticism	• Appreciation
• Feeling unsafe	• Feeling secure
• Limited view	• Broader view
• Human Normal	• Human Spirit

It's pretty clear which type of relationship would make any of us happier. Now ask yourself, "Am I being all of those things in my relationships?" If you find yourself wishing your partner resembled the list on the right, I have great news for you! You have the power to bring out the best in others, or you can bring out the worst. I spent so many years failing forward (and backward and sideways) in relationships before I learned the exact solutions that I'll be teaching you in this book. Relationships are hard, and none of them come with an instruction manual. Considering that most of these hurdles are also invisible, we may not even realize they are there. No school subject has ever covered how to be in a relationship, so we tend to learn by trial and error. Ouch! When I shifted how I showed up in relationships, my entire world took a quantum leap forward. I am truly wishing for a similar, spectacular result for you!

Human Normal and Human Spirit — Self-Reflection Questions

- When do you see yourself in Human Normal?
- When do you see yourself in Human Spirit?
- What is your favorite way to shift into Human Spirit?
- With what challenges or specific situations do you find it hard to shift into Human Spirit?
- What does your partner's being in Human Spirit provide for you?

(Now ask them the same question!)

Two

Hunting Mode or Gathering Mode?

I have learned that human beings have these two different ways of operating that we can call Hunting Mode and Gathering Mode. We can think of these as two separate operating systems, just like in a computer. Think of Mac and PC laptops, which outwardly look very similar. They both have keyboards and screens. There are a couple of things outwardly that look different; however, all in all, they look very, very similar. Yet, on the inside, we know that these two operating systems work very differently, and some would even say they're incompatible. Each operating system has its own strengths and weaknesses, and the same is true of Hunting Mode and Gathering Mode (as I'll be referring to them throughout the rest of the book).

Here's the difference between the two. Whenever we have a result to produce and there is a deadline, we're in Hunting Mode. When we don't have specific time constraints or tasks that must get done, we are more likely in Gathering Mode. People have the ability to switch back and forth at any time and may prefer the

> Whenever we have a result to produce and there is a deadline, we're in Hunting Mode. When we don't have a specific time constraint or tasks that must get done, then we are more likely in Gathering Mode. People have the ability to switch back and forth at any time...
>
> BARBARA COLE SALMERON

mode that is more dominant for them. As a business owner, I am a woman who is in Hunting Mode a lot! My husband and I agree that he is in Gathering Mode more often than I am. So, let's explore the differences between the two modes, some of the conflicts that arise, and how to heal or even prevent these common misunderstandings. Because truthfully, wouldn't we all enjoy a life with less conflict?

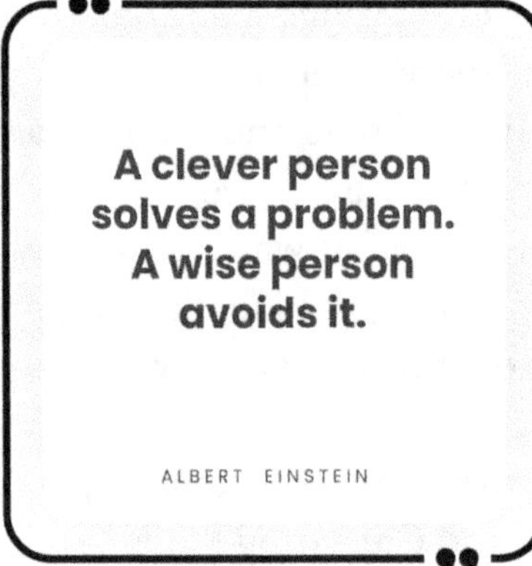

> A clever person solves a problem. A wise person avoids it.
>
> ALBERT EINSTEIN

Hunting Mode

When a person is in Hunting Mode, they are committed to producing a specific result, intention, or destination. This could include finishing a work project before the deadline, getting to an appointment on time, or getting dinner on the table by 7 p.m. Hunting Mode always involves a time constraint, which increases our level of focus. In fact, we can become so focused on the result we are producing that we may not notice when someone enters the room or begins speaking to us! We screen out anything that is irrelevant to the result we need to produce.

Remember, women don't usually achieve Single Focus due to our lower testosterone and higher estrogen; however, we can have a very high level of focus when in Hunting Mode. There are plenty of times when I've been working on a big deadline and my husband comes into the room to tell me something. When I'm deeply focused, I often don't hear him at first. Once I notice that he's talking to me, I look up and say, "I'm sorry, honey, I didn't know you were talking to me. Could you please repeat that?" You may have noticed not being heard when approaching a person who is in Hunting Mode. It can be more effective to say the person's name first and wait for a response if you think they are in Hunting Mode, especially when it's a man, considering his superpower of Single Focus.

How to Tell When Someone Is in Hunting Mode

Here are some indications that someone is in Hunting Mode: When walking, they're typically moving quickly and in a straight line, literally speaking. They will use the shortest, most efficient route possible to get where they're going because they're on a deadline, after all! There's no meandering, and often, their head is down because they are still focused on producing *their* result. When working at a computer, their head is likely down, and they will be more impatient if they are interrupted than when they are not in Hunting Mode. Can you see it?

You may also hear them say "I think" rather than "I feel," and they will likely reference facts and statistics. Their speaking will be short and to the point — sometimes just a one-word answer! This can be perceived as rude, or we might think they're upset with us when, truly, they are just in Hunting Mode and focused on producing their result. This can cause significant conflict at work, at home, or in romance, especially if the other person is in Gathering Mode and wants to connect on a deeper level.

The Cave People Analogy

Why do we call this Hunting Mode? And why do people sometimes get so irritated with interruptions? When they feel that frustration, it is their Human Normal instinct rising up because, back in the day of the cave people, the hunters and warriors had some very important results to produce. They needed to feed the tribe or protect the tribe, and a failure to deliver those results, sadly, meant that others died! Back then, men were typically the hunters and the warriors because, due to having significantly more testosterone than women, they had larger, denser muscles, allowing them to run faster and be physically stronger. The women were generally the nurturing caretakers and took on the roles of gatherers, handling many tasks at once to keep everyone fed and healthy.

In modern times, we obviously don't have the same threats to our survival; however, those ancient neural pathways still remain in the human brain — meaning we are always on the lookout so we can protect ourselves and our loved ones. The person in Hunting Mode *feels a sense of safety when they are producing a result.*

The person in Gathering Mode, which we will explore next, feels safe when experiencing a connection to others. This mode was important in earlier times because we had to live together in groups to survive, so having a sense of belonging and being liked and accepted by the group were a matter of life and death. To be cast out of the group was dangerous — especially for a woman — as she would then have to find or build her own shelter, hunt for her own food, and protect herself and her children if she had any. This led to a particular subconscious behavior of women wanting to please others, or at least avoid displeasing them. Ladies, we know how we sometimes bend over backward to keep everyone happy, right? Of course, we want our loved ones to be happy; however, we also want to steer clear of conflict to avoid getting kicked out of the tribe! This is another example of our survival instincts acting to protect us from a perceived threat. Because the male and female brains are structurally different, some parts of my teachings will be specific to men or women, while other parts will relate more to the human condition.

> **The purpose of Hunting Mode is survival, and producing a result helps us to think we are safe.**
>
> BARBARA COLE SALMERON

Today, many of us, myself included, tend to feel a sense of anxiety or unrest when we think we didn't get enough done in a day. Our to-do lists are impossibly long, and it seems to be human nature to focus on the one thing we didn't get done rather than the one hundred things we did complete. I believe this links back to our survival instincts (rooting back to the way the cave people functioned) around feeling safe when we've succeeded in accomplishing an important result. Have you ever noticed how good you feel at the end of a productive day? I know I find it easier to relax after a day of accomplishment compared to when I don't get much, or "enough," done. Can you feel the judgy self-criticism there? This is a sign that Hunting Mode is likely my default! Many societies definitely value productivity. So much emphasis is placed on it, but to the detriment of having a personal connection with others — and yet, we truly need both productivity and connection in order to live our happiest and most fulfilling lives.

The purpose of Hunting Mode is survival, and producing a result helps us to think we are safe.

Gathering Mode

When a person is in Gathering Mode, the survival instinct is connection. In Gathering Mode, we are open to options, alternatives, and possibilities. There are no deadlines or time constraints, and it's more of a free-flowing state.

Remember from the section But First … It's All About Testosterone! that women have a superpower called Diffuse Awareness. It's important to note here how the inner landscape of a woman's brain differs from a man's. I have described it to my husband in this way: it feels like one hundred channels in my head, all playing at once, 24/7. If you are a woman reading this, you know *exactly* what I'm talking about! If you are a man reading this, it probably sounds unbelievable or even a little crazy to you. Welcome to our inner world!

All of this brain chatter, by the way, is why we *don't believe men* when we ask what they are thinking about, and they respond by saying "nothing." That feels utterly impossible for most women. It also sounds very peaceful, enviably so. Ladies, our men can have an *empty box* inside their head where they go to think about nothing! Please note, I'm not saying their head *is* an empty box, but rather, they can *have* an empty box tucked away in there. We attribute this difference to a man's superpower of Single Focus (due to having higher testosterone and lower estrogen) and a woman's superpower of Diffuse Awareness (due to higher estrogen and lower testosterone). Because Diffuse

Awareness has a woman noticing anything and everything in her environment; we believe it is what causes multitasking. Not only is the female brain capable of multitasking, but also *we often are unable to stop it.* Back in the day of the cave people, our survival depended on it, and it is still a very strong muscle in the female brain.

However, as women in Gathering Mode, we can also feel very overwhelmed by our Diffuse Awareness. When everything is calling out to us all at once for our attention, we find it harder to prioritize. It's often more difficult for us to decipher which thing is a priority because they all feel equally important to us in Gathering Mode. Someone who is in Hunting Mode, especially a man with his superpower of Single Focus, might say "Well, just prioritize" or "Just do the most important thing first." Yet, in Gathering Mode (which is about connection rather than productivity) and with our Diffuse Awareness, everything feels equally important and *past due.* It can be very difficult to know what things to tackle first, which brings about that sense of overwhelm. With all the responsibilities of work, family, health, friends, chores, and so on — all feeling past due — how can we prioritize? This often leads to women putting their own needs last to make sure everyone else is taken care of. No wonder so many of us feel exhausted much of the time; it's tiring just to think of it all!

Here's a tip for the men (Ladies, share with them!). I heard this many years ago from my sister: When her husband did the dishes, it was like foreplay for her! Why? Because it gave her a chance to rest and regain some energy after a long day, perhaps saving some of that energy for the bedroom! Now, isn't that a win-win? In my masterclass called Orgasm vs. Intimacy (Series 1–8), and perhaps in a future book, I talk about what women need to be open and available for sex. So, guys, romance her by letting her rest, taking care of a few chores, and observe what changes!

How to Tell When Someone Is in Gathering Mode

When we are in Gathering Mode, we move more slowly. We're not rushing because there is no deadline. This could be when we are cooking a nice leisurely dinner or maybe we're taking a well-deserved relaxing bubble bath. When walking, we're more likely to be looking up, smiling, and making eye contact rather than keeping our heads down. Our walking will be more of a stroll, as there is nothing specific to be accomplished at that moment. We take time to stop and smell the roses.

The person in Gathering Mode has greater access to patience. We're able to experience compassion and feel more open. Our speaking will include more detail than that of the person in Hunting Mode, and you may hear us say "I feel" more often. You can also tell when someone is in Gathering Mode because they are asking about you. They're asking "How was your day?" or "How'd your meeting go for you today?" When they ask about you and about your day, they are seeking out connection and attention. This adds value to our human relationships and can bring warmth to our interactions. Connection is the survival instinct that compels the person in Gathering Mode, as it helps them to feel safe.

> **The purpose of Gathering Mode is survival, and connection helps us to feel safe.**
>
>

The purpose of Gathering Mode is survival, and connection helps us to feel safe.

The Cave People Analogy

Women, as gatherers, did a lot of tasks back in the day, such as going out into the meadow to collect berries, firewood, or medicinal plants. Women were, of course, responsible for the children and probably also had to build fires to keep the tribe warm and cook the food to provide nourishment to everyone. There was a lot that women were (and still are) responsible for to keep everyone in the tribe healthy! Our Diffuse Awareness had us observe and communicate in tremendous detail to avoid danger.

While gathering in the meadow, we stayed together in groups for safety, and we talked endlessly to help shoo away the critters. If we were to startle a critter, it might scratch us or bite us, and back then, that was a life-and-death situation. There weren't any antibiotics or hospitals, so a bite from even a small critter could be serious or even fatal. So, to let the critters know we were coming, we'd move in groups and talk and talk so they could get out of our way. Have you ever met someone who talks and talks as if their life depends on it? They are likely in Gathering Mode. Now you know where this comes from!

Communicating in tremendous detail was important. Let's say I knew where the good berries were, and I knew they were going to be ripe this afternoon; however, I had to stay behind to build the fire and watch the cave kids. So, I would then need to communicate plenty of detail to my fellow cavewomen as they went out into the meadow to collect and gather. You see, the good berries looked almost identical to the poisonous berries! I had to make sure that the women picked the good berries and not the poisonous ones because that could really harm a lot of people in the tribe. Can you feel the tension building behind this survival instinct? I would need to let them know that the poisonous berries are on a bush that always grows down by the river, and the leaves on that bush are green and glossy. The good berries grow on a bush with thick and fuzzy leaves, and this bush can always be found up on the hill, never down by the river. Oh, and the good berries will be ripe this afternoon, and if they aren't picked before sundown, the birds will get them instead of us.

Do you see the amount of detail needed? Again, this was a matter of life and death. I interviewed a married woman named Carrie, who made this connection between romance and details: "Maybe this is why women love writers and poets — they are communicating with lots of words!"

Also related is the concept of safety in numbers: Have you ever noticed that women tend to go to public restrooms in twos or in groups? My theory is that safety in numbers is where this behavior comes from, too! Ladies, do you notice that you tend to visit the same bathroom stall each time it's open? That's because we know that stall is "safe" *on a subconscious level;* there's no *tiger* hiding in that stall! We also tend to feel safer in certain groups, so we form cliques with people we trust, and we don't share our secrets (our descriptions of the berries) with others we don't trust or don't know. Can you see how some of our modern-day behaviors may have their origins in our ancient survival instincts?

Which Is Better?

Remember, the Hunting and Gathering Modes are like two different operating systems that we all have access to. Both are valuable, and each has its own inherent strengths and weaknesses. In most things, I refrain from labeling something as good or bad just because it is different. This allows me to be more open and curious about the differences and how they can be of benefit, rather than assuming they are a detriment. The human brain is hard-wired to automatically notice food, danger, and attractive people — all as part of our natural survival instincts. It's easy to see how food and danger impact our survival, but attractive people? Yes, on a subconscious level, our brain looks for the top combination of traits to give our offspring the best chance of survival. We subconsciously look for a mate who is attractive, strong, and intelligent and who possesses resources (money, power, stability, and so on), all so our *future imaginary children* can best survive! Now you know why tall, dark, and handsome men get so much attention from the ladies. Remember, *it's not logic; it's instinct.*

Our brains will also classify something (or someone) who's *different* as *danger* and *similar* as *safe*, which is why we can feel uncomfortable when doing something new for the first few times. I believe this also contributes to racism, war, and many kinds of conflicts. Our brain tells us to fear that which is different from us, creating an *us versus them* mentality. In the past, it was warring clans; today, it is warring countries, religions, families, and — sadly — relationships.

So, who's hunting, and who's gathering? In our decades of research since

> **The human brain is hard-wired to automatically notice food, danger, and attractive people — all as part of our natural survival instincts.**
>
> BARBARA COLE SALMERON

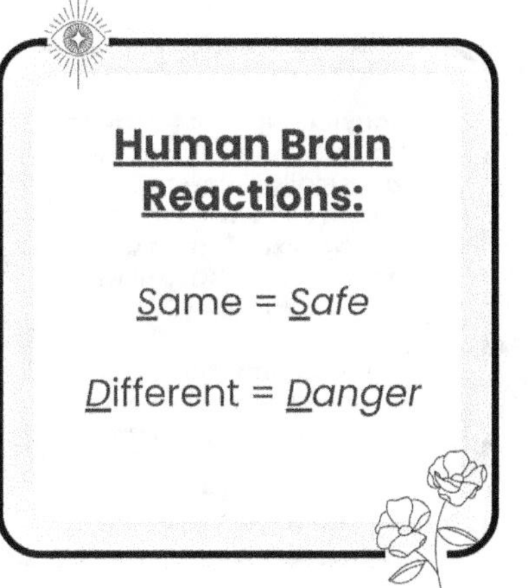

1991 (among myself, my mentor, and colleagues), we've found that women tend to go back and forth a lot between Hunting Mode and Gathering Mode, depending on the situation, what is needed, and whether there is a time constraint. Most men, on the other hand, spend the majority of their time in Hunting Mode until after the age of about fifty, and that is mostly related to their much higher testosterone levels (the fuel for getting things done!). As they age, their testosterone declines, and it gets *easier* for them to access Gathering Mode and express their feelings!

Many of my teachings have to do with biology and the huge roles that testosterone and estrogen play. Please make sure to read (and revisit) the section. But First … It's All About Testosterone! at the end of the Introduction. Considering that the male and female brains are physically different since before birth, why on earth do we expect men and women to behave in the same way? These expectations are *so invisible* we don't even notice we have them! Not knowing about our actual biological and brain structure differences, and not realizing that we likely have invisible expectations of the opposite sex, it's no wonder that we struggle to understand each other. And nobody teaches us this stuff! Until now, that is. Please remember to go easy on yourself and those you're in partnership with because human beings don't come with an owner's manual, and it's natural to be confused by the opposite sex.

Consider this list of behaviors triggered by survival instincts and which mode they show up in. In my books and masterclasses, I teach about each of these more in-depth:

> **Considering that the male and female brains are physically different since before birth, why on earth do we expect men and women to behave in the same way?**
>
> **These expectations are *so invisible* we don't even notice we have them!**
>
> BARBARA COLE SALMERON

Other Ways Our Survival Instincts Show Up:

Hunting Mode *OR* Gathering Mode ❓

Hunting Mode	Gathering Mode
• Purpose: Survival	• Purpose: Survival
• Compelled to: Produce results	• Compelled to: Connect with others
• Speaks: To the point	• Speaks: Lots of details
• Focus	• Diffuse Awareness
• Time constraint	• Timelessness
• Competition	• Collaboration
• Facts	• Feelings
• Respect	• Attention
• Solving problems	• Relativity
• Concealing	• Revealing
• Conserving	• Including
• Behind the plan	• Behind the person
• Dishonor	• Betrayal
• Legacy (in parenting)	• Reflection (in parenting)
• Orgasm	• Intimacy

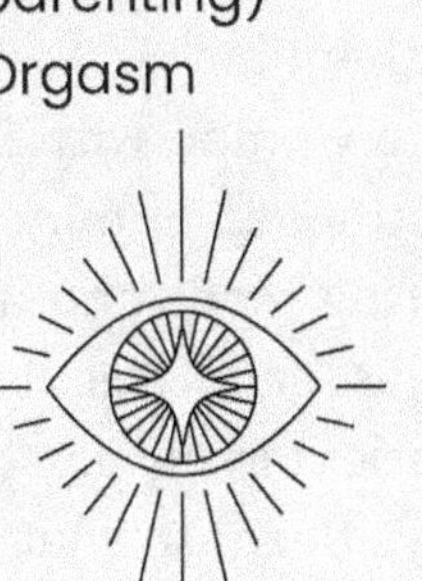

Which ones do you see in yourself? And in your loved ones? The point here is that *none of these are wrong!* It is my goal in these teachings to illuminate and celebrate these differences in each other so that we can truly transform the battle of the sexes into peaceful, abundant, juicy, loving, and productive partnerships full of respect and appreciation.

Student Example

When I was recording this masterclass, one of the students was my boyfriend (now husband), Rick. We both agree that I am in Hunting Mode most of the time, and he is in Gathering Mode more often than I am. Even in his work, he is often in Gathering Mode. Women are drawn to hire him as a financial planner and wealth manager because his style and personality are very comforting to them. As you will read in Chapter 6, feeling "safe" is crucial for women and is a prerequisite to feeling "happy," especially feeling safe in the area of finances!

Rick mentioned that he feels he is in Gathering Mode often, so I asked him to expand on that for the class, and he shared these insights:

It's the moments when I want to connect with people that I find myself more in Gathering Mode. I want to open up a conversation and just chat for a while and spend time with them to get to know them better. I wouldn't say that I notice everything like a woman with Diffuse Awareness would; that's not a strength of mine at all. But some of these other Gathering Mode characteristics I feel like I can relate to. See, I just said, "I feel"! I like to think I'm more patient than impatient in my personality. That's something that I've always been, so that seems to be natural to me. I find myself in Hunting Mode while

> working, for sure, but I do feel more comfortable when I'm in Gathering Mode.

He brought up a great point here in that the different personality traits that each of us has will influence this. Some people feel more comfortable in one mode or the other, and we all have aspects of both modes. If Rick and I made each other feel "wrong" for being in opposite modes so often, our marriage would really be on the rocks! And I can honestly say that if I hadn't learned the material that I'm now certified and licensed to teach and share here with you now, I would have self-sabotaged this relationship just like I did all the others.

> If my husband and I made each other feel "wrong" for being in opposite modes so often, our marriage would really be on the rocks!
>
> And I can honestly say that if I hadn't learned this material … I would have self-sabotaged this relationship just like I did all of the others.
>
> BARBARA COLE SALMERON

Can you see how conflict occurs when one person is compelled to produce a result, and the other person feels compelled to connect? Both people just want to feel safe, and neither person is wrong. Just this foundational piece of my teachings can cause misunderstandings and hurt when not known. Can you see where you have *important relationships* that are often in opposite modes? I hope this illuminates what might be happening behind the scenes, allowing for a true opening to understanding and embodying grace for both people.

I've created a fun video for you that explores how two common activities, grocery shopping and driving, look in Hunting Mode versus Gathering Mode! Check it out at BarbaraColeSalmeron.com/Books.

Hunting Mode and Gathering Mode — Self-Reflection Questions

- Do you relate more to Hunting Mode or Gathering Mode?
- When do you see yourself showing up in Hunting Mode?
- Where do you see yourself being in Gathering Mode?
- Does this concept bring you clarity on someone else's behaviors?
- How can you show up differently when in a Hunting Mode/Gathering Mode conflict?

Three

The Worth-It Calculation!

Now, let's take a deep dive into something happening behind the scenes with men. For some men, this part is very obvious. Others have not given it much thought, but they generally agree when they hear me describe this.

So, what is the Worth-It Calculation? It is something that's happening in the background for men constantly and it's how they decide if a job, a relationship, or any choice they are about to make is "worth it" *or not!* Sometimes, they'll go through the calculation in a split second, or sometimes it will take a few minutes. Some Worth-It Calculations could

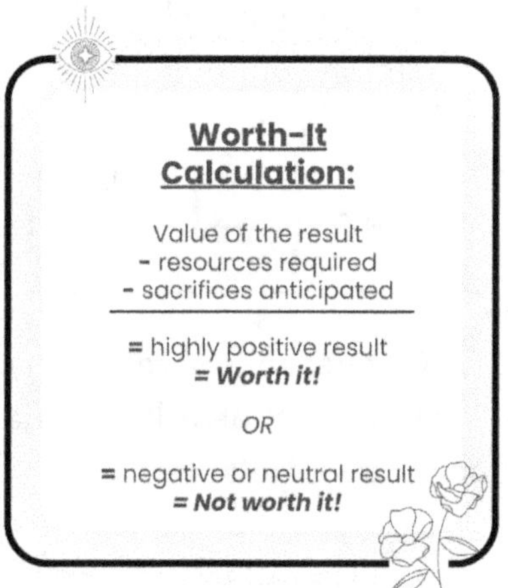

take hours or days because the goal or the project they are considering is that big. The Worth-It Calculation is constant and it's automatic for them. Sometimes the men in our lives don't even know that they're doing it or that it's happening. But you can start noticing it when you're talking to a man and you've asked him a question, or you've asked him to consider doing something; the Worth-It Calculation will be going on.

I asked Rob in Texas what things in his life *are worth* his effort, and he said, "Keeping my marriage happy, staying closely connected with my family, and keeping up healthy life pursuits, such as ways to make sure that I'm in growth mode rather than decaying."

I asked Carl in California the same question, to which he replied:

It has to fit in with my vision and goals. I'm growing my business but also maintaining and growing my partnership with my girlfriend, Simone, and my friendships. It's a balancing act between the two because sometimes I might want to work all night. I'll be working on blogs or on my book, and I just want to work until ten or eleven at night, but that throws my partnership with Simone out of balance. So, when it's five o'clock, I'll stop working and spend time with her, and maybe we'll go out to take a walk on the beach. We'll talk the whole time and feel connected. So that's worth it.

Our decades of research with men have confirmed that this is what the Worth-It Calculation looks like for them. The variables are as follows:

- The *value* of the result/outcome (meaning the impact it had, the difference it made, what he provided, or what problem he solved — generally for the person requesting the outcome)

- Minus the estimated time, energy, and money that it will take
- Minus the sacrifice anticipated (which means what they won't be able to do while they're working on this objective, like missing out on a sporting event or some hard-earned downtime)

If that calculation works out to have a high positive number or result, then he deems this request, task, or project to be *worth it.*

If it's a negative or a neutral result, or maybe just slightly positive, he's going to deem that it's *not worth it.*

Again, this goes back to our survival instincts. If you were a hunter, and you're expending more energy out there hunting while not bringing back

Side Rant! Please note that when *either* sex feels something is "obvious" or "common sense," that means the opposite sex is probably clueless about it! This is part of what causes so much conflict in our relationships because, again, the male and female perceptions and thought patterns are very different. Many of us fail to see these differences and we certainly don't learn about this in school. I am convinced that once you gather more examples of the information I'm about to share, you will gain clarity about how to improve your relationships!

I like to say that men and women are like fish and birds: a fish will never know what it's like to take those long flights across the sky, and a bird will never understand what it feels like to breathe underwater. We are *that* different, and what is obvious to one sex is often *breaking news* to the other! Again, these teachings are based on over three decades of research interviews with men and women.

the big game, it's a waste of resources and a threat to the tribe's survival. If you brought back a rabbit that won't feed everyone versus something much larger, then you're expending more energy than the value of the result, and ... it's *not* going to be worth it. See the connection to our survival instincts?

> The Worth-It Calculation is happening in the background for men constantly, and it's how they decide if a job, a relationship, or any choice they are about to make is "worth it" or *not!*
>
> BARBARA COLE SALMERON

I asked Kevin, a retired man in Texas, how his Worth-It Calculation has changed over the years. He shared that before he retired, money, comfort, and job satisfaction were most important to him. Kevin said, "In my post-retirement stage, my biggest passion is performing comedy. I have no expectation to get cash out of it. But the satisfaction and joy that I get out of it is off the charts. So, it's a no-brainer for me." I met Kevin in a stand-up comedy class, and at this stage in his life, comedy is something *worth doing*. Through Chapter 7 and Chapter 8, we'll dive into the stages of development of men, and you will see how their Worth-It Calculation changes through the different stages.

There is something powerful that can change the balance of the Worth-It Calculation. It's the receiver's *shown appreciation* that can change everything! Now, *shown* appreciation is not just "Oh, he knows I appreciate it" or "I'm pretty sure he's aware that I appreciate it." Appreciation needs to be intentionally expressed and not just assumed. The appreciation expressed is not only for *what* he did but also in *a way he can receive the expression*. Similar to the concept of the five love languages,[3] men will interpret your expression of appreciation in different

---

[3]   Gary Chapman, PhD, *The 5 Love Languages: The Secret to Love That Lasts*, December 11, 2014, Northfield Publishing.

ways. This requires you *asking him* what appreciation looks like for *him.*

It's a great conversation to have with the men in your life because this is going to be different from man to man. Some men love a verbal acknowledgment that what they provided was beneficial for you. Telling them what their efforts *provided for you* is also especially meaningful to most men. Men may also wait to see if you use, in some way, what they have provided. I've found a great way to show appreciation is by praising a man in front of others. Public acknowledgment can be very powerful!

You can ask the men in your life, "What's the best way for me to show you my appreciation for all of the things you provide?" That is a deep question and a great conversation starter! The shown appreciation can *increase* the value of the result for him, or it can *decrease the feeling* of the money, energy, or time he sacrificed and expended. For example, if he initially thought that on a scale of 1 to 10, the value of this result is a 7, but then appreciation is shown, it can make the value jump up to a 12! Or that appreciation can make the energy and sacrifice he made seem much less significant, and therefore, the exchange is *worth it.* Our *shown appreciation* can really change everything!

It's a game changer — apply this shown appreciation more regularly, and just watch the changes come trickling in for the better. In my research, I asked Carter, a married man in his forties, if appreciation was important, and what it provided for him. He said, "Absolutely. When I feel there's enough wood on the fire to fuel my efforts, I'll do it. I've realized more and more that appreciation is a kind of fuel in our personal and professional lives."

> There is something powerful that can change the balance of the Worth-It Calculation.
>
> It's the receiver's *shown appreciation* that can change everything!
>
> BARBARA COLE SALMERON

Rob, a married father of two, shared this when I asked what appreciation provides for him: "I feel appreciated and recognized. It provides a sense of satisfaction, joy, and happiness. It's the flowers of that garden that I put time and effort into, and appreciation is the fertilization to produce a healthy garden." For him, appreciation is a two-way street and makes his second marriage *worth it.*

In our research, we've found that the Worth-It Calculation can also apply to women who spend a lot of time in Hunting Mode. I can certainly see that when I use logic and my conscious mind to make a decision, such as by writing a pros and cons list, I want to figure out if something is *worth doing!* The area where I don't see the Worth-It Calculation as much is when I'm making an emotional decision, or I'm focused on pleasing (or avoiding displeasing) someone. We see so much of this when we, as women, agree to something we really didn't want to agree to and later wish we hadn't!

Men have a different point of view on this, especially later in life when they are compelled to live by their values. You can tell what someone's values are based on by observing where they spend their resources (money, energy, and time). I asked Tom, a man in his fifties who is nearing retirement, what makes doing things for others worth it, and he said, "With most of my friends and family, it's just worth it. For strangers, it's because they're human beings. My grandfather and my dad raised me that way. You protect your family and others, especially those who are unable to protect themselves. Period. And no matter what the consequence. It's in the DNA. I just need to ensure that people are taken

> **A man's Worth-It Calculation need not be set in stone. It can be influenced by new, factual information and experiences.**
>
> BARBARA COLE SALMERON

care of." Can you see the "protect and provide" instincts in Tom's statement?

A man's Worth-It Calculation need not be set in stone. It can be influenced by new, factual information and experiences. Such was the case with Rob when he shared the following:

Getting married again for me was knowing that my marriage is something that I need to focus on, spend time with, and not take for granted. It means showing appreciation for everything that my wife does for me, which takes energy and effort. I can't just take it for granted. The cost of committing to a vow, to promise forever — that's a big cost. It was something I told myself I'd never do again, and that was a big hurdle. The turmoil and bad feelings from my previous marriage made doing it again *not worth it*, in my mind. But having my marriage now is a far higher value than the energy it takes to be married. This kind of support system is great. It's fantastic, and we wouldn't have gotten there, at that level, if we weren't married. Something like marriage is a big commitment, and you don't get that from being boyfriend and girlfriend.

The Worth-It Calculation — Self-Reflection Questions

- Where do you see the Worth-It Calculation happening for the men in your life?
- When, if at all, do you see the Worth-It Calculation in your own decision-making?
- Can you think of times when you didn't understand a man's decision about something? Did this chapter help to explain it?

Four

Facts versus Feelings

The person in Hunting Mode usually relies on trusted facts that are actionable. Christopher, a married man in Texas, had this to say about facts: "Until verified, I'm not convinced it's a fact, and I do not act on something until I know it is a fact."

And Christy in California, who is also in Hunting Mode most of the time, shared her perspective: "In science, there is no fact; there are just theories. I was raised to believe that 'they' were telling us facts, but I was rebellious … I had my doubts. I trust seeing and feeling, not being told. Why would I trust anything out there? Medicine and food are making us sick. The media

> **When someone is speaking, we can discover the person's values and what is important to them, as well as who or what they trust.**
>
> BARBARA COLE SALMERON

manipulates that information, but they are supposedly feeding us 'facts.'"

A fact, to someone in Hunting Mode, especially a man, means information from a trusted source. When someone is speaking, we can discover the person's values and what is important to them, as well as who or what they trust.

We can often decipher who or what is a trusted source for someone who is in Hunting Mode because the information from that source appears as fact to them. Beth in Texas said this is how she determines who is a trusted source for her: "I get a 'feel' for someone after spending time with them and observing them and seeing if their behavior matches their words."

You'll notice that I refer to my mentor, Alison, a lot in my material. As my teacher and mentor, she is a trusted source for me. I have learned her material, experienced its value, put it to the test in my own life, and have had results far beyond anything I could have imagined. So, to me, Alison is very much a trusted source!

John, a consultant in his fifties, described how something becomes a trusted source for him as "something that I can verify, other than my own gut reactions, which I have also come to trust." Carrie, a mom in her forties, said, "I am my most trusted source. I check in with my gut. If it does not feel right to me, it doesn't matter what the evidence says; I will do what feels right to me." Carrie is a woman who spends lots of her time in Gathering Mode. She's delightful. She also really trusts her gut, intuition, and feelings. We will explore the topic of gut instinct next!

Whenever you listen to someone speak, listen for their values and what is important to them. For a person in Gathering Mode — in this case, for women — we have a very different relationship with our feelings than men do. When we hear someone say "Feelings are not facts," that can really ruffle our feathers! Feelings, for most women in Gathering Mode, are very real. For women, feelings are a valid and important way we process information, interact with others, and make decisions. Christy in Los Angeles shared, "If I am feeling something, it feels like a fact, especially in the heat of the moment! But once processed … I find it is not as overpowering. As adults, our culture wants us to stuff emotions and not express them, so instead of processing them, we eat, drink, shop, lie, cheat, steal, and f***!"

With most men in Hunting Mode, feelings are not considered a trusted or tested source; men often view them as too abstract and therefore not actionable. John describes it this way: "Feelings are choices. One can choose to be happy, angry, elated, and so on. Once we choose to feel a certain way, then all sorts of things surface. Feelings are not facts." Again, the distinction between a feeling and a fact is not right or wrong; it's just one of the *innumerable ways* that men and women differ in how they think, behave, and experience life!

> **With most men in Hunting Mode, feelings are not considered a trusted or tested source; men often view them as too abstract and therefore not actionable.**
>
> BARBARA COLE SALMERON

Gut Instincts

An exception to not seeing feelings as facts is the "gut feeling." This *can* be acted upon. This is why people share how they followed their gut feeling or their gut instinct, which was not something that felt difficult for them to follow, nor did they need to have a particular source to verify — the gut feeling in and of itself can be a trusted source.

Have you ever ignored your gut feeling or those red flags and later regretted it? Lana in Texas shared, "Both men and women can ignore [red flags] when we are in a new relationship." So true, especially when the physical attraction is incredibly strong!

In my research, I've seen that as we age and gain life experience, we tend to trust our gut more and more — especially if we've ignored it in the past and experienced negative consequences. John in California had this to say about gut instinct: "I have learned to trust my own gut reaction. It gives me input that I used to ignore, to my own detriment. I have learned to follow it, even if I don't know why. I have driven 2,000 miles to be somewhere that I felt I needed to be, even though I didn't know why. It all lined up, so now I trust my gut instinct."

Christy put it this way: "I trust my gut, my intuition, my inner knowing."

Christopher in Texas also commented on the concepts of gut instinct and trusted sources. He said, "If what I am seeing does not mesh with what I think is right, with my gut instinct, experience, or principles, it takes an overwhelming amount of evidence to sway me."

Tammy in California shared, "I trust my first response on something as far as intuition and gut instinct. When I blurt something out without thinking, it does usually turn out to be the truth."

Rob, a married dad of two teenagers, said, "My relationship with my gut instinct is a good one. I believe it is a strong source, an accurate source, most of the time."

My dear friend Tina in Michigan, a mom of two, stated, "I don't second-guess my gut; I just do it!" She taught me how important gut instinct is to a mother. She had an experience with her first child where she disagreed with a doctor. The clinic staff tried to talk her into following the doctor's advice, but she said it just didn't feel right, so she stood her ground, even though she was young and inexperienced. And it turns out she was right! Unfortunately, women experience this over and over in Western medicine, as most of the historical research and medical studies were done *only on men.* I go into more detail on this in my bonus chapter on women's health, which can be found at BarbaraColeSalmeron.com/Books.

Last, my favorite quote on gut instinct comes from my husband, Rick. He said, "I had a good gut instinct that you were an amazing person, both before we met and even stronger now. I would not have picked you up at the airport the day you arrived in Dallas had I not had a gut instinct that you were worth picking up. My gut told me *This is going to be worth it!*"

I'm so glad he trusted his gut instinct!

Can you hear the subtle differences between the male and female perspective? Can you tell who is coming from Hunting Mode versus Gathering Mode? I promise, once you start to see these subtleties, you won't be able to *unsee* them! This greater awareness brings us the freedom of choice — we can choose to react in the same ways we always have, or we can choose to come from curiosity and compassion instead to create a new result.

With the gut now being called the second brain, it seems as if science is starting to explain the phenomenon of why we have such strong gut

> **Your gut has capabilities that surpass all your other organs and even rival your brain. It has its own nervous system, known in scientific literature as the enteric nervous system, or ENS, and often referred to in the media as the "second brain."**
>
> EMERAN MAYER, AUTHOR OF *THE MIND-GUT CONNECTION*

feelings, which also feel very true and easy to trust. A woman may equate this to following her intuition; however, if you are speaking to someone in Hunting Mode, they will more easily relate to following their gut or gut instinct. So, whenever a person feels unsure about a decision or what path to follow, it's best for them to follow their intuition and gut instinct to help ease them into taking action.

Trusted Source — Challenges for Women

Can you think of any areas in your relationships where you're not an expert? For example, my husband is a financial planner and wealth manager, and even though I used to be an accountant and owned a bookkeeping company, he is the expert on protecting and growing our wealth. It would be silly of me to think I could give him advice on investing unless that was something I really studied or had a passion for. In our marriage, I am not a trusted source of money advice, and I'm OK with that!

With some couples, one parent might be more of an expert on the kids' activities or school life, so the other parent will consider them a trusted source and defer to their judgment *on those issues*. Unfortunately, it can be a challenge for a woman in Gathering Mode to be seen as a trusted source by the men in her life or by anyone in Hunting Mode. This is because the two main factors that contribute to becoming a trusted source are consistency and congruency.

Consistency is about showing up in a way that is less sporadic and more grounded and also rooted in a clear pattern of behavior. For someone in Gathering Mode, this can be hard because we are so dynamic and adaptable that we can shapeshift and change our focus, our opinions, and our minds easily. This is seen as inconsistent by the person in Hunting Mode.

Congruency comes from our words, feelings, and actions. Ideally, all three of these are aligned. If they aren't, we won't be seen as having integrity — we could even be seen as less trustworthy.

One way that the person in Gathering Mode can help to demonstrate consistency and congruency is to own up to their experience of changing their mind. Rather than not acknowledging a change of mind, we could clearly communicate and say "I want to share that I know changing my mind right now seems like inconsistency — I'd like to acknowledge that and explain why I have changed my mind and feelings on the matter." Simply stating this can go a long way to building trust! Men change their minds, too, when something is verified by facts or when there is new information from a trusted source.

Lana shared her thoughts on finding a trusted source: "It's getting more difficult to tell what is true these days. I have to depend on the source; what is their agenda? Who is paying for that research? When money is involved, too many people put their interests above helping others."

Can you see where you are a trusted source in your relationships? Can you see where you might not be?

Thinking, Facts, and Opinions

When someone is in Hunting Mode, you'll hear them say "I think ..." For example, they'll say "I think I'm safe" or "I think I'm financially secure." They are coming from a place of *thinking*. So, here's a tip for you when communicating with someone in Hunting Mode: consider saying "I think" to match the mindset they are in — they could be more likely to receive and even *trust* what you have to say. You could also say "In my experience ..." or "It seems ..."

Often, the person in Gathering Mode will say "I feel this" or "My feelings about this are …" And this is true for us — we do *feel* that! However, it's common that others in Hunting Mode won't relate to that and may find it hard to connect with what you are sharing. Experiment with the above suggestions and see what the results are!

When it comes to opinions, we can ask a woman "What is your opinion on global warming?" And there will often be a fast answer from her, especially if she's in Gathering Mode. Even if we've never thought about it or read anything about the topic, we still tend to share instantly and say things like "Oh, it's awful" or "It's because of this … and we need to do that …"

However, for men in Hunting Mode, their opinions are very subjective. They will use their life experiences — including their values, the people and places they respect, and all they've learned throughout their entire life to form such opinions.

For a woman in Gathering Mode, when she gives her opinion, it can be like "Here's my opinion, but I might have a different opinion tomorrow or this afternoon, yet for today, this is my opinion."

It's completely different for men! They are very invested in and thoughtful about their opinions, which they often *see as fact*. I'm *not* saying that women aren't thoughtful, because we most certainly are! Women, especially when in Gathering Mode, just have a different relationship with their feelings, which can cause our opinions to shift.

With a man, instead of asking for his *opinion* (which is a heavier, more loaded word in many cases for some men), we can ask for *advice* or *input*. We can say "This is what *I think* will solve the problem. What *do you think?*" In this case, we have to be really careful because sometimes *advice* is the keyword, and sometimes it's *opinion*. Ask the men in your life how they define *advice* versus *opinion* and which one carries more weight. Ask them, "If someone doesn't follow your advice, what is that like for you?" You may well be surprised at the answer! We will go deeper into men and their advice in Chapter 8.

Gathering Mode and Feeling Safe

All of us have many different levels on which we evaluate whether or not we feel that we are safe. Sometimes, we can have a *feeling* of safety even if we're actually not safe. We can also *feel* unsafe in a situation when we actually are. There is emotional safety and physical safety — it's complex, I know. So, when we consider the topic of feeling safe, what does it mean? And is it based on facts (as determined by someone in Hunting Mode)? Pay attention to whether you sense a difference between *feeling* safe and *thinking* that you are safe. What would someone in Hunting Mode trust more? In Chapter 6, we will explore the six dimensions of safety for women in further detail.

Another interesting aspect of feelings is that women, especially, tend to have their *most* favorite feelings and their *least* favorite feelings. Feeling happy, fun, attractive, and intelligent — these could be some of a woman's favorite feelings. It's different for every woman, of course! Christy, a woman in her forties, told me that among her favorite feelings are "humor because it creates the ultimate connection and feeling wanted, sexy, or capable."

On her *least* favorite feelings, Christy said, "I hate feeling shamed, not good enough, belittled, or judged." This is also different for everyone and is based on our experiences, the way we were raised, and what insecurities or fears we may still carry with us. Discomfort could arise from things like feeling worthless, invisible, stupid, or ugly ... you get the picture.

Something for you to consider is what your most favorite and least favorite feelings are. This is interesting when it comes to dating ... Many of us will choose to date people based on how *we feel* when we are with them. Do they help us feel our favorite feelings?

If a man brings out her favorite feelings — like feeling beautiful, intelligent, and fun on a first date, she will be more likely to want another date with him because she loves how she feels when she's with him.

Now, the opposite is also true in dating, especially if she's on a date with someone who leaves her feeling unintelligent, not valued, or unattractive. She probably won't even want to go on a second date with that man. Perhaps this is where ghosting was invented?

> If a man brings out her favorite feelings — like feeling beautiful, intelligent, and fun on a first date, she will be more likely to want another date with him because she loves how she feels when she's with him.
>
> BARBARA COLE SALMERON

Ladies, we must also think about how our words and actions affect the men in our lives. Do they experience being loved, respected, and appreciated? Or do they think they've been criticized? Judged? Misunderstood? There are many little ways that we tend to *unknowingly* disempower or even emasculate our men! Some of those ways include a certain "look" or a tone of voice, interrupting them, criticizing them in front of others, and yes, even reloading the dishwasher after he's already done it. Even if we don't say a word, the message we send is "You didn't do that right." Tammy in California saw this in her own life, and she shared with me, "My mom emasculated my dad all the time, and I saw him as shrunken, with stooped shoulders, later in life."

Have you ever had a friend or coworker whom you could never please? Eventually, didn't you stop trying since it felt like everything you did or said was wrong anyway? This is exactly what happens to the men we love! So, eventually, they stop trying, then they stop speaking, and then we wonder why they're quiet and distant or why our relationship feels on shaky ground. Carl, a divorced father of two, describes his experience this way:

> I was so unaware, I kept in it when my marriage was so, so bad. I now know with my ex-wife, I was just constantly getting emasculated. But I didn't know that's what it was, you know. I didn't know that those feelings I was having, all those negative, crappy, crummy feelings I kept having was because she was emasculating me. Or she was manipulating me as she was lying to me. I just thought it was me; I thought it was my problem, right? Why am I feeling like shit all the time? She kept telling me I'm a bad father, I'm a bad husband. And I kept believing her.

This is a very extreme example of emasculation within a relationship. Unfortunately, the subtle ways we disempower each other are far too common and create so much conflict in our relationships.

To the men, these emasculating or disempowering behaviors are *obvious*, and they think it is *also* obvious to us — yet this is not so! Just as what is obvious to the female brain is *not at all* obvious to the male brain. We think they "should know" or we might then assume they are misbehaving in some way. However, remember our two core questions: What if there's a good reason for that? And what if no one is misbehaving?

> To the men, these emasculating or disempowering behaviors are obvious, and they think it is *also* obvious to us — yet this is not so!
>
> Just as what is obvious to the female brain is *not at all* obvious to the male brain.
>
> BARBARA COLE SALMERON

Think about how much you want to provide or be there for a loved one who leaves you feeling disrespected, dishonored, or demeaned in some way. It doesn't exactly inspire love, loyalty, or openness, does it? Our men can experience being disrespected even when we don't think we are being critical. I had to learn this the hard way with not only lovers but also a few friends. I used to think I was being "helpful" when I was actually being critical.

Years ago, I heard it said this way at a conference: "Unsolicited advice is criticism!" My Human Normal instinct rejected that idea until I truly let it sink in. Even though my intention was to be helpful, it was often *not received that way* at all. I even lost a few friendships because I was clueless about how my input was being received. When men are repeatedly criticized for doing things differently from women, is it any wonder that men withdraw, become quiet, or feel like they *just can never win* with us? Have you ever felt that way with someone? I know I have!

Respect is critical to the person in Hunting Mode, and we will explore that further in the next chapter. For now, I will leave you with my number one piece of relationship advice: *Replace criticism with appreciation!* Even if someone loads the dishwasher "wrong," I invite you to smile, thank them for their contribution, and walk out of the room if you can't keep yourself from "fixing" it. Give it a shot and see how things change — you'll start to see a world of difference, all in favor of a healthier, happier relationship!

Facts versus Feelings — Self-Reflection Questions

- What are some of your favorite feelings?
- What are some of your least favorite feelings?
- Do your feelings seem factual to you in certain situations?
- How do you determine what is a fact?
- Who or what is a trusted source for you?
- What causes you to lose trust in someone?
- What is your relationship with your gut instinct?
- Where have you been unwittingly criticizing others, and what has been the result?
- What are some steps you can now start taking to create a different result in your relationships?

Five

Respect versus Attention

As we examine respect versus attention, we'll see how this applies to both professional and personal relationships. If you've ever had the feeling of being disrespected by someone, you know how awful that feels! Similarly, if you've ever felt like you're not getting enough attention from your honey, you may have felt triggered without really knowing why. In this chapter, we'll explore how respect and attention are tied to our ancient survival instincts and how crucial they are for happy partnerships at *home and at work!*

Respect and Hunting Mode

When we're in Hunting Mode, respect gives us our greatest access to being productive. This means that when we're working with other people, they choose to work with us because there is mutual respect. Together, we can create a more powerful result, which can be much bigger than what we could ever produce on our own.

Why? We have more resources, brainpower, energy, and support. Forming those associations and strategic alliances can really help us be more productive (even if you like to work on your own — there are still areas that could benefit you to collaborate with others). We can simply produce a much greater result when working with others!

Consider someone in Hunting Mode who is not respected. Their results become limited to what they're able to produce on their own. They have limited resources and energy. For people in Hunting Mode, respect is as serious as "life or death." Imagine back when hunters banded together in groups to go after a large animal.

There was a level of respect for one another, as well as for the group effort, in order for them to all work together. If one man was an outcast and not respected for some reason, then his hunting and providing capacity would be severely limited. He would have been left chasing after rabbits instead of hunting the big game. Since hunting (a form of providing) equals sustenance and survival, this is where the life-and-death feeling comes in. *Expending too much effort for a very small result violates the hunter's Worth-It Calculation!* Can you see it? We expanded on the Worth-It Calculation in-depth in Chapter 3.

> Consider someone in Hunting Mode who is not respected. Their results become limited to what they're able to produce on their own.
>
> They have limited resources and energy. For people in Hunting Mode, then, respect is as serious as "life or death."
>
> BARBARA COLE SALMERON

Our modern-day people in Hunting Mode still have this biological instinct to place a high level of importance on respect, even if it doesn't directly relate to survival in the same way that it once did.

When the person in Hunting Mode is not included or invited to join in group collaborative projects and events, especially at work (which is their source of providing for themselves and others), it can feel like a threat to their livelihood.

When thinking about the people in your life, you can understand what respect means to them personally by *asking them*. Some illuminating questions are "What's your experience of being respected?" or "What does respect look like to you?" It can be too easy to *assume* that everyone experiences respect in the same way, yet that's not true at all! For example, do you feel disrespected when someone is late for a meeting with you? What if it happens again and again? Many people experience being disrespected in this scenario.

However, is it *possible* that someone's tardiness is more about their own time management issues rather than blatant disrespect? As a person with a neurodivergent brain (one that works differently from an average or "neurotypical" brain), I speak from experience here! This is another area where we can think something is *obvious* or *common sense*; however, just because someone thinks a behavior is disrespectful doesn't mean that everyone agrees with them.

Tammy in California said this about respect during my research interview with her: "Respect makes me feel buoyant and more alert. My brain is in gear, as well as my feelings. Both sides of my brain are engaged. I am happy, safe, on solid ground, protected, and encouraged to move ahead on my own."

John, a consultant in his fifties, expressed himself this way: "Lack of respect is not just life and death; it is an overpowering sense of isolation as well. Feeling isolated reduces productivity, and isolation feels dangerous; like not belonging, it is life-threatening."

Without experiencing respect from the people who are most important to us, we can find ourselves in the middle of a caveman or cavewoman attack, also known as a meltdown! Next, let's look at how to avoid that scenario.

How Do You Experience Respect?

In my own research, I've asked hundreds of people how *they* experience respect. Most women say that they feel respected when people are honest with them, when they feel heard and valued in their opinions, and when they are included in decision-making. Women also feel respected when their boundaries are accepted and their feelings are honored without judgment. Beth, a stepmom of two, said this about respect: "I feel respected when my opinion is asked for and valued, when I am listened to, and when my feelings are accepted, understood, and not dismissed or invalidated."

Lucy, a single woman in her thirties, shared her views on how respect and integrity go hand in hand for her: "Respect for me is about being honest and truthful with both the good and the bad, and also when the other person is open to my suggestions. Respect equals integrity. When I respect a person, I believe them to be a person of integrity and someone I can count on. Being truthful is an important part of that."

The men I interviewed shared that they experience respect when they are accepted for who they are. Also, being invited and included, experiencing a sense of camaraderie, being asked about their ideas when part of a group, and even hearing words of affirmation or praise can feel like respect for many men.

Ladies, you know how we crave to feel loved and adored? Check this out: *Respect is to men what love is to women*. In our decades of research, men have told us again and again that when they experience being respected, they feel loved. Imagine that! Respect in the workplace communicates to them that they are liked, appreciated, and acknowledged. Respect at home feels like love, support, and appreciation. This concept of respect is so very important to men *and* to women in Hunting Mode. Never underestimate the immense value of telling and showing your respect to those you love! Most importantly, *ask* others how they experience respect! As we have seen, respect is perceived differently by everyone. Without asking, you may think you are showing respect to someone; however, it might not be received that way.

Eleanor in Texas equates feeling respected to feeling safe. She said, "Safety in a relationship ties into respect for who I am. I have a big fear of losing my identity within a relationship; that feels very unsafe to me."

Maggie expressed her perspective this way in our research interview: "Respect looks like someone being willing to spend the effort to listen to what I have to say, to honor my feelings without judgment, and to be willing to talk openly, with appreciation, while honoring me."

Attention and Gathering Mode

In Gathering Mode, receiving attention is our best way to access feeling connected and therefore safe. When we receive adequate attention from the people who are

> **When we receive adequate attention from the people who are important to us, we feel connected to them.**
>
> **Remember, connection equals safety at the instinctual level!**
>
> BARBARA COLE SALMERON

important to us, we feel connected to them. Remember, connection equals safety at the instinctual level! This makes the person in Gathering Mode compelled to seek out attention in order to "survive," just like the person in Hunting Mode seeks respect for the same reason. Beth, a divorced woman in her forties, told me about her inner experience:

When I am not getting enough attention from my partner, I find myself getting more needy. I need more verbal reassurance and deeper conversations, and I have an insatiable need for time. I felt that in my first marriage, and we just couldn't figure out how to fix it. My tank was so empty. If I feel disconnected from my partner due to lack of attention, I tend to have mood swings or spend a lot of time in sadness and really mentally fixate on the sadness.

Beth also shared with me what it feels like when she does get enough attention from her partner. She said:

I feel so relaxed and calm. I feel safe and secure. I feel loved, valued, and supported in gigantic ways that I have never experienced before. I feel like the toxicity of stress has left my body, leaving me feeling more capable and confident than ever before!

Can you relate?

Back in the cave people days, women were reliant on bigger, stronger males to be the providers and protectors. It was, and still is, simple biology which dictates that men have larger, denser muscles and can run faster because of their *much higher* testosterone levels. Women also needed to feel connected to the rest of the tribe to share skills, cook, be taken care of when unwell, and even get help with raising children. So, a lack of connection with our providers (men) and the rest of the nurturers (women in the tribe) would be a life-and-death situation. As women, we developed the behaviors over time of *pleasing*, or at least *avoiding displeasing*, as a way to feel liked, connected, and safe. In modern-day life, this can look like not wanting to step on anyone's toes, and we potentially hold back from expressing our true feelings and needs out of fear of being judged, rejected, or losing connection. It's also why we so often say yes to someone when we really want to say no. Sadly, this instinct keeps so many women from speaking their truth and asking for what they really need.

When we are in Gathering Mode, receiving attention is a very big way for us to feel connected to others. An example in modern times is receiving a message back from someone whom we recently emailed or texted. That provides us with a sense of safety. So, what happens when we send an email or text and *don't* get a reply?

First, we might check to make sure the message was sent, and then maybe we check to see if they read it. With no response yet, we reread it and wonder what is wrong — did we offend them? Should it have been said in a different way? Are they mad at us? Where did we go wrong? Oh, the stories we make up can eat away at our insides! Carrie, a married mother of five, shared this with me: "My husband will sometimes take days to answer an email that requires more thought. He's thinking about it, and I can feel nervous about why he hasn't answered yet."

In reality, we have no idea why they haven't responded. It could simply be that they are busy and want to respond when they have more bandwidth. When we feel that we are not getting the attention or connection we need, we're more likely to respond with concern or anxiety because our Human Normal survival instinct has been triggered. Remember, back in the day of the cave people, if someone didn't like you and you got kicked out of the tribe, then that would be a death sentence for almost anyone, and most especially for women! Those instincts are still deeply entrenched in the human brain.

Now imagine if that was our boss who didn't quickly respond to the email. It's easy to start making up all sorts of stories and assumptions, and pretty soon, we've convinced ourselves that we're going to be fired. Sound familiar? This would trigger our (financial) safety survival instincts and could lead to a caveperson attack (a meltdown) really fast!

Of course, we do this in our personal relationships, too. If our honey is late getting home and not responding to calls or texts, our imaginations can really run wild. Did their phone die or get lost? Were they in a car accident on the way home? Are they having an affair?! The stories we make up can take us into a downward spiral of dread.

In a romantic relationship, if the person in Gathering Mode isn't getting enough time or attention from their partner (perhaps they work a lot), they typically won't feel safe. It will become very difficult for that person to be in the relationship if their partner is not providing the attention they need and crave. Carrie shares how physical touch can fill her need for attention: "When I get revved up about something, my husband will touch my hand or my back, and it soothes me. It is a grounding thing! But he needs to be focused on me; otherwise, I don't like it."

There are different types of attention: connection attention (spending time together or talking on the phone), intellectual attention (in groups of people socially or at work), and sexual attention (receiving compliments or being flirtatious). If you are like me and really value quality time, then receiving enough connection attention, especially from a romantic partner, can make or break the relationship!

This can even happen with friendships. I've personally had to end a few friendships with people who did not reciprocate the time and energy I was putting into the relationship. And that's OK! For me, it was about setting healthy boundaries with people whom I found to be very draining (who always had

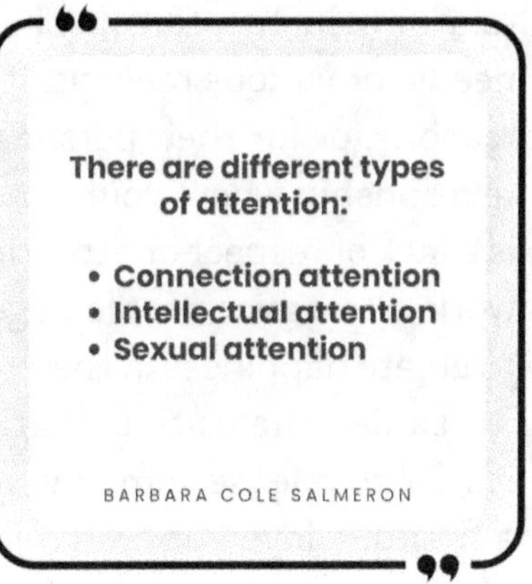

lots of drama or chaos in their lives), and who were never there for me when I needed them anyway.

By ending those friendships, I released the drama and gained peace, which happens to be one of my highest values. It's perfectly OK to release toxic relationships of any sort. In reality, women often have a hard time closing the door on toxic relationships because they long to "make it work" and because our survival instinct tells us we must, above all, please others or avoid displeasing them. It's no wonder walking away sometimes feels uncomfortable!

This story, told to me decades ago, illustrates an aspect of how women can sometimes stay in a relationship for far too long. The mother of one of my best friends is a divorce attorney. My friend said that when a man walks into her mother's office and says he wants to file for divorce, her mother asks him to do a few things, like trying marriage counseling for several months. After that, if he still wants a divorce, she draws up the papers. But when a woman walks into her office and says she wants to file for divorce, this attorney draws up the papers. To me, this story illustrates that once a woman is done, she is *done!* She's tried everything in her power to make it work, stayed too long out of guilt, and eventually reached her breaking point. Ladies, do you relate? Men, too, can stay in relationships that don't meet their needs for various reasons. It could be for the kids, for financial reasons, or for their personal beliefs about divorce. Being in a relationship where your needs aren't being met or where there is a lack of respect or attention is misery. My intention with this work is to assist people in getting their needs met (and more) to create happiness in their romantic relationships and beyond!

Ladies, the truth is that we *can* survive on our own now, so it's OK to release someone who is not meeting our needs, be it a friend, a lover, or even a job. I know it can be scary to think of making a big change (remember, our brain already thinks *different = danger*), yet truly, if you are in a relationship or a job that doesn't meet your needs, then consider what life would be like if the opposite were true. What could you accomplish, or who could you be in the world, if you knew all of your needs were met? The relationship tools that I share with my clients and students show them how to create loving partnerships where everyone's needs are met with ease and joy!

Let's now return to the concept of attention as we explore how the reactions to intellectual and sexual attention will vary from person to person, depending on their life experiences and personality. The person might be very comfortable and encouraged by it, or such attention might elicit strong feelings of *not* being safe. This could look like *not* speaking up in front of a group when asked for your opinion, especially at work (intellectual attention), or through a man's direct gaze or whistles when you are walking down the street (sexual attention). Yes, guys,

> **What could you accomplish, or who could you be in the world, if you knew all of your needs were met?**
>
> BARBARA COLE SALMERON

we can *feel* that, even if we don't make eye contact, and it can often feel very creepy!

For some women, this attention will feel like a compliment; for others, it will feel like disrespect, and for someone with any kind of sexual trauma in their past, it can feel downright dangerous. The wrong kind of attention — especially from the wrong person — can absolutely trigger our survival instincts. Christy, a single woman in her forties, shared this about certain types of attention: "I don't like attention from authority or management. I prefer to be under the radar, not on center stage. I also feel safer with a one-on-one connection over being in groups."

We all have different needs in terms of the attention that helps us to feel safe and what causes us to feel unsafe. Questions that can help us understand our partners better include "What forms of attention do you love?" "Who makes you feel safe when you receive attention from them?" and "What kinds of attention leave you feeling unsafe?"

Lucy in Texas described a first date where too much attention left her feeling unsafe: "I am not comfortable with too much direct attention. I dated someone who counted how many times I chewed my food. He was a police officer, so maybe he was trained to notice details. He stared at me and told me exactly how many times I chewed my food. I thought, *Wow, that's very specific,* and it felt like I was under a microscope. I only went on two dates with him!"

For someone in Gathering Mode, attention and safety are also about noticing when you're worrying about how someone feels about you. Notice how you don't feel safe and secure when you question what someone thinks or feels about you. Examine what kind of attention you need and what happens when you don't get that attention. What kind of attention do you need to feel safe, and what kind of attention makes you feel unsafe? When we don't feel safe because of a lack of attention or connection, we are definitely not at our best! I know for myself, my capacity for patience and compassion toward others is drastically decreased when I'm feeling unsafe or disliked in some way. Making decisions based on fear rarely brings us the result we're seeking. So, when you feel that instinctual Human Normal tension rising in the body, breathe, pause, and shift into Human Spirit before making important decisions!

When a person is in Gathering Mode, they are asking for connection through attention when they ask "How was your day?" "What happened at your meeting?" and so on. They are seeking safety and connection through the attention of conversation, and they likely want to share the details of their day with you. As a woman in Hunting Mode most of the time, I can feel annoyed at having to think back about my day and recite the details. This is because the person in Hunting Mode sees it as a waste of resources (money, energy, or time) to repeat the details of their day. However, it's never a waste if talking about your day creates connection with someone you care about, as it *provides* so much for them. Remember, the person in Gathering Mode typically only shares their details with people they trust!

Wrap-up: The person in Hunting Mode needs respect to feel safe, whereas the person in Gathering Mode needs attention. Perceptions of respect and attention vary wildly from person to person, and the lack of these things can trigger our ancient survival instincts. Over time, our need for respect and attention can be the demise of important relationships, especially when we don't know how to address our concerns or how to ask to get our needs met. Remember, this isn't logic; it's instinct!

> Making decisions based on fear rarely brings us the result we're seeking.
>
> So remember to breathe when you feel that instinctual Human Normal tension rising in the body, pause, and shift into Human Spirit before making important decisions!
>
> BARBARA COLE SALMERON

Respect and Attention — Self-Reflection Questions

- What things do you experience as disrespect?
- What things do you experience as respect?
- What does being respected provide for you?
- What happens when you don't receive enough attention?
- What does receiving attention provide for you?
- What are your favorite types of attention?
- What are your least favorite types of attention?

Six

The Six Dimensions of Safety

This chapter speaks more specifically about women and how we experience being safe and secure. Safety and security have to do with both thinking and feeling, and we'll see how they affect us in both ways. This will make a lot of sense to the ladies, as most of us can relate. It'll also be very enlightening for the men in your life!

Experiencing being safe in these six different dimensions is typically a *prerequisite* for a woman to be able to be *happy.* It's the foundation she needs for the higher Human Spirit states such as happiness, joy, compassion, peace, patience, and laughter. It's very difficult

> Experiencing being safe in these six different dimensions is typically a prerequisite for a woman to be able to be happy. They are:
>
> - Physical
> - Mental
> - Emotional
> - Financial
> - Spiritual
> - Temporal (Time)
>
> BARBARA COLE SALMERON

for us to be in those elevated states if our foundation of being safe and secure is not there.

Beth had this to say on the topic: "When I feel safe, I am a lot less needy in a relationship! I feel safe when my partner does what he says he's going to do, and when I feel he has my back."

Maggie experiences safety in this way: "To me, safety is knowing there is someone I can depend on regardless of how stressed I am, and they are willing to just let me vent and then say 'OK, we can fix this!'"

Let's explore the six different dimensions of safety because it's not just about being physically safe! Since physical safety is the most familiar, we'll start there.

Physically Safe

With physical safety, a woman is asking herself whether she is in a safe neighborhood or whether she feels safe with the people around her. Women are *subconsciously* monitoring their safety in any situation or setting, which is much different from how our men experience it. Much of this has to do with the parts of the brain that process fear and how these parts interact with other parts of the brain. As you now know, the male brain is structurally different and responds differently than the female brain does. Current medical research shows that women are much more likely to experience classically defined fear, anxiety, and depression than men are.[4,5,6] For the ladies, this can create many silent worries, which we often do not voice. For the guys, in the day of the cave people, we needed our men to have *less*

---

4   "Depression in women: Understanding the gender gap" by Mayo Clinic Staff, Mayo Foundation for Medical Education and Research (Online resource)
5   "How Anxiety Affects Men and Women Differently," Texas Health Resources (Online resource)
6   "Fear: Men vs. Women" by fearlesspsychology, May 25, 2018. Fearless Psychology (Online blog)

fear because it allowed them to go into battle to "protect" and hunt to "provide."

In our research interview, Lucy said this about safety: "I feel physically safe when I am with people I know and trust. Also, when my nieces and nephews are safe, their safety makes me feel safe; the world is OK."

And Carrie shared her perspective, which was largely influenced by her experiences during childhood, as it is for most of us! She said, "When I am helping, I feel safe and secure because I am feeling valued. Others will keep in touch with me, not forget me, and I won't be left to starve!" Being ignored is scary for her. She felt invisible as a child and was afraid of being forgotten. She gets physically sick to her stomach thinking about being forgotten.

Mentally Safe

Mental safety can be experienced in women's thought patterns. For example, is she feeling good about life? Is she having good thoughts about it? This is one of the places where *thinking and feeling* (Hunting and Gathering Modes) are combined. If she doesn't feel mentally safe, what would that look like? She could be feeling mentally tired, confused, or not understanding what's happening around her. She could be with people with whom she feels it's not safe to express her thoughts, such as with strangers or in a difficult or unsupportive work environment, so she stays quiet and suffers in solitude.

This lack of mental safety could make her withdraw and feel disconnected from others, which leads to a greater sense of feeling unsafe. Have you been in situations where it felt safer to *not* speak up? I know I have! On the other hand, we all know what it feels like to be in a relationship with someone who is not very present or attentive. It's not fun for anyone, and the relationship itself either ends or drags on for years with both people feeling unfulfilled. Do you have friends whose romantic relationships look like that? In the workplace, mental withdrawal decreases job satisfaction, productivity, and longevity in a position. Employers know that staff turnover and training of new hires ultimately can hurt the bottom line, so ensuring that their female employees feel safe is *critical* to running a successful organization.

Carrie, who is in Gathering Mode most of the time, relates to mental safety in this way: "I crave more detail when something is being asked of me, and I also give a lot of detail. Not having a lot of detail puts me in a state of feeling mentally unsafe." Remember, the person in Gathering Mode communicates with much more detail than the person in Hunting Mode. Without *communicating* all that detail, the person in Gathering Mode feels like something *terrible* is going to happen, such as someone bringing home poisonous berries!

Christy shared her perspective on mental safety: "When I am around someone with too much ego, I do not feel safe. My doors are locked. Where is my money, and where is it going? Where my stuff is matters because all things in [their] place means mental safety for me. I need to have others around me who think like me so I know I'm not crazy!"

> **Without *communicating* all that detail, the person in Gathering Mode feels like something *terrible* is going to happen, such as someone bringing home poisonous berries!**
>
> BARBARA COLE SALMERON

Emotionally Safe

Being emotionally safe has to do with both the emotions that the woman is experiencing and her thoughts about those emotions. If she was raised in a family or in a culture that says women are *not allowed* to feel angry, then when she feels anger, she may have thoughts such as "I'm not supposed to be feeling this," "This isn't appropriate," or "I have to be careful to not express my anger because if I do, there will be consequences." This is where the Hunting and Gathering Modes can also get combined. She's experiencing emotions, and then she's having thoughts about them, perhaps judging herself against cultural norms and seeing herself as wrong (even though she's not!) for feeling the emotion of anger, which then can fuel her guilt.

If a woman doesn't feel emotionally safe with someone, she could again withdraw and put up walls of self-protection. This happens when she has been belittled or invalidated for her emotions or not supported in some other way. When I was younger, I used to "joke" that I was so good at building walls (emotional walls, that is) that I should own a construction company! This might sound familiar to you if you've experienced being emotionally unsafe. Being supported emotionally is so important for women, and we often turn to our girlfriends to talk it out or think out loud — basically, being allowed to vent can feel very therapeutic for women.

Here's the problem, Ladies. Our men, who are in Hunting Mode most of the time, don't usually have the capacity to listen to all of the details that we feel *compelled* to share! Most men *and* women in Hunting Mode need us to get straight to the point or the problem so they can help us "fix it" and then get back to the result they need to produce elsewhere. And then we get annoyed with them for offering solutions rather than just

> If a woman doesn't feel emotionally safe with someone, she could again withdraw and put up walls of self-protection.
>
> This happens when she has been belittled or invalidated for her emotions or not supported in some other way.
>
> BARBARA COLE SALMERON

listening! Does this sound familiar to you, Ladies? I have a pre-recorded masterclass, and perhaps a future book, on this exact problem called *Speaking to the Point and the Problem* (Series 2–5) at www.Grow.BarbaraColeSalmeron.com.

Ladies, ask the men in your life what *their capacity* is for long monologues with lots of detail. If they feel *safe enough* to tell you the truth — meaning that it *won't* be held against them later — then they will answer you, usually in the number of minutes they can handle. As for their wanting to "fix it" when you just want them to listen, it's really not fair to them! Men are natural-born problem solvers, and Ladies, most men won't spend time or effort solving problems for someone unless it's a person they care about. So, if he's wanting to offer solutions, it's because *he cares!*

There's no use talking about the problem unless you talk about the solution.

BETTY WILLIAMS

Learning how to speak to men in a way they can *best* hear you will increase your chances of being understood a thousandfold. Short and to the point, without all the details, is what will work best for most men — and for women in Hunting Mode! If they need more details about the situation, they will ask for it. Until then, the old adage of *less is more* applies here. Can you see how this also applies to our success in the workplace?

On emotional safety, my coaching client Rob said, "When my wife doesn't feel safe, she cries, becomes more introverted, and speaks in lower tones, as opposed to my ex-wife, who is more of a thunderstorm, which caused me to withdraw like a turtle in order to protect myself."

And Carrie in Texas shared, "It's nice to have the money, but the emotional safety is more important to me. I will sleep in my van if I don't feel safe at home!"

Financially Safe

Financial safety is a really big one! This can be a *huge trigger* for our "inner cavewoman" because it *literally* feels like a life-and-death situation to us. Again, we're talking about instinct here rather than logic, and these instincts are deeply ingrained in the human brain. Women can feel their survival is threatened when they feel financially unsafe. Elements of time will also influence feeling financially safe in terms of past, present, and future. For instance, how long has she felt financially safe, if ever? Does she feel good about her current income or job security? Does she think she's saving enough and on track for retirement?

If she's someone who grew up with financial security, she might not give this area of her life much thought. However, if she's had financial struggles for most of her life, she could feel financially unsafe even if things are better for her now. I speak from experience on this one! I want the men to know that women experience a lack of safety in a very real, *very visceral* way, especially when it comes to finances!

> **I want the men to know that women experience a lack of safety in a very real, *very visceral* way, especially when it comes to finances!**
>
> BARBARA COLE SALMERON

I interviewed John, a consultant in his fifties in California, who said, "When a woman feels unsafe financially, oh man! They fear for themselves and their kids not being taken care of. They seem to operate as if they are constantly at risk and are worried about everything, which gives way to scarcity behaviors. It really opens up Pandora's box of ugliness."

Now, that might sound harsh; however, this is *his* experience of women when they don't feel financially secure. Many women I have interviewed express a similar sentiment, such as Lucy, a student of mine who was in my class on the dimensions of safety. She shared: "It feels like I am, right now, in that space of financial fear because I don't have a job. I took money out of my retirement; I made stupid decisions. My employment is ending next month, and I'm feeling like the world's ending! *What am I going to do? Oh my gosh!* That's me right now, and it's been me for a long time."

Beth in Texas experiences it this way: "A lack of financial stability creates anxiety and constant worry for me. I'm always thinking about plan B rather than being in the moment."

Eleanor, a woman in her forties, had this to say: "As a single mom, safety was knowing that I had a job and I did not need to rely on anyone else. Having the job, being good at it, and giving time to it so I could advance."

Can you feel how financial insecurity can trigger a survival instinct? Remember, it's not logic; it's instinct!

How is this experienced differently by men? Let's take the example of my husband, Rick. Financial security is his line of work! He caters his business to helping his clients have an experience of safety and feeling comfortable and taken care of. Rick will tell you from his professional experience that most men are all about the bottom line, the numbers, and the rate of return. That's a very different outlook from wanting to feel safe and comfortable with the person who's handling your money and keeping an eye on your retirement. All in all, these are two very different aspects that he sees again and again in men and women.

Spiritually Safe

This dimension has to do with the woman's own spiritual and religious beliefs. Does she feel supported in this area? Is she part of a spiritual or religious community that she feels good about and supported by? Does she feel a connection with her higher power or with the other people in her life? This is a very personal yet important area that can help her cope with life and calm the storm when she's feeling unsafe in any of the other dimensions.

If she's not a religious or spiritual woman, then her local community or volunteer work might be where she looks for fellowship because she can be of service to other human beings in this way. Helping other people can bring us a higher sense of satisfaction and connection and truly help us feel fulfilled and safe. Remember, feeling connected to others reassures the woman's survival instinct that she's OK, on a very subconscious level. Who is your "modern-day tribe" to whom you feel most connected?

Beth shared with me what spiritual safety feels like for her, saying, "Spiritual safety for me comes when I am being regular with meditation, deep reading, and other spiritual practices I engage in. Religion is the opposite of spiritual safety for me, as women are still viewed as 'less than' in most religions."

Temporally Safe

Time-related safety was a big one for me personally! This is when the woman looks at her calendar and sees how overly packed it is. Does she have enough free space in her calendar? Is there any white space at all, or is it just crammed full of appointments?

We've all had days like that, especially around the holidays or other super busy times of the year. Can you feel the exhaustion?

I used to be so bad about this. I would not even give myself time to drive and to eat! I would schedule back-to-back appointments and forget about the fact that I actually needed to eat a few times a day. I used to have what I would describe as a time phobia, just for lack of a better phrase.

I called it a time phobia because I was constantly overbooked, overextended, and completely overwhelmed. I would just run around all day saying "I don't have enough time. I don't have enough time. I'll never get this all done!" And in truth, I wouldn't be able to get it all done! I'd be exhausted by the end of the day, and then the next day, I'd do it all over, again and again. I was constantly exhausted and stressed after several years of over-booking myself, and I actually damaged my health. I developed severe adrenal fatigue, which took years to recover from. Please don't follow my example!

Beth in Texas also shared, "I feel unsafe and panicky when my day or week is just packed too full. Ultimately it is my self-care and health that suffer when I am facing a challenging schedule."

If you've ever felt that way, just take a deep breath and see where you can fit some white space in your calendar. It's OK to say no sometimes!

> I was constantly exhausted and stressed after several years of overbooking myself, and I actually damaged my health.
>
> I developed severe adrenal fatigue, which took years to recover from.
>
> Please don't follow my example!
>
> BARBARA COLE SALMERON

Remember, our instinct to please and avoid displeasing is alive and well, and we honor it far too often when we should be honoring our own needs instead. It will benefit our physical and mental health to have some free time scheduled into our day. Don't be like me and forget to eat while working until midnight every day. It's important to carve out some time and space to ensure our health and wellness. Oh, the glamorous life of a solopreneur!

These dimensions of safety are also affected by our past, present, and future. I've created another short bonus chapter for you all about that, which can be found at BarbaraColeSalmeron.com/books.

In summary, when a woman experiences being safe and secure, we can bring out the best in her with a lot less effort and with fewer obstacles. She'll be able to access her overflowing reservoirs of patience, compassion, and affection. When we're in a cavewoman attack, we're not as capable of displaying those things until we stop and take a few deep breaths to shift ourselves into Human Spirit.

Dimensions of Safety — Self-Reflection Questions

- Where do you see examples of physical safety in your life?
- Where do you see examples of emotional safety in your life?
- Where do you see examples of mental safety in your life?
- Where do you see examples of financial safety in your life?
- Where do you see examples of spiritual safety in your life?
- Where do you see examples of temporal (time-related) safety in your life?

Seven

Men's Development — Early Stages

When we're empowering the men in our lives, we're also empowering ourselves. Doesn't it make sense that we will get the best from men when we help them feel empowered?

However, I must warn you: if we use this information to manipulate men, it will backfire.

If we use this from a place of empowering men while also empowering ourselves, then this information can sit in our readily available toolbox, helping to truly transform our lives. It's an incredible and different point of view that will equip us with some powerful knowledge that, perhaps, you never knew existed before now.

We can produce increasingly better results for ourselves in every aspect of our lives, including our businesses, organizations, families, and education, by understanding the stages of development for our magnificent men! Do you want more loving, connected, and respectful relationships and partnerships in your life? Who doesn't, right? I encourage you to learn this material and expand your knowledge based on what I'm about to share. You'll reap the rewards you've been longing for in your relationships!

We'll dive into three key areas (plus more juiciness):

> **We can produce increasingly better results for ourselves in every aspect of our lives, including our businesses, organizations, families, and education, by understanding the stages of development for our magnificent men!**
>
> BARBARA COLE SALMERON

- What men are generally focused on in each stage of development
- What support men need, specific to each stage
- What the Worth-It Calculation looks like in every different stage

To the degree that *we women* are operating from Hunting Mode, we, too, can go through some variation of these stages. Paying attention to how we can relate to these experiences can help to deepen our understanding of men. Now remember, we're not attempting to *change* the men in our life to fit our own liking. The goal here is to recognize their behaviors and relate these to their stage of development.

The variety of experiences in each stage can help men to understand their own internal drives and outward actions, as well as empower women on how to best be in partnership with them. Men reading this section can also see these stages in the *other men they know*, helping to create a deeper understanding of where there may currently be confusion or frustration.

Warning: We never want to *tell* a man what stage he is in! We can ask him to read about the stages or give a quick synopsis

(I put a summary together to assist with that at the end of the book — you're welcome!) and then *ask him* which stage *he thinks* he is in. We might have our thoughts about it, but it's not up to us to decide that for him. Instead, use your power of compassion for the men in your life during these chapters, keeping in mind they're only human and mostly running on instinct, just as we all are!

Page

Let's talk about the first stage of development, which we call the Page. This refers to our little guys from birth to puberty. Note that the timing of the stages is approximate because men are going to shift through these stages at different ages depending on many factors, including their personal life experiences. Some may transition to the next stage earlier than others, so know that any ages I give are more of a general guideline.

The focus of our little men in the Page stage is to have adventures and test themselves. They are little Knight wannabes (the next stage), but they're not quite ready for Knighthood yet!

The Page is all about adventure by way of testing themselves to sort out what they can and cannot do. Even though it's not as obvious, they are already aiming to protect and provide for the people they love. Ask a little boy to *help* you with something and praise him for being your *hero*. See him smile and puff up with pride. It's remarkable!

Now, the protective instincts are innate in most men at any stage. Men are, instinctually, natural-born *providers and protectors*. They want to provide for and protect the people who are important to them — the people who are in their "realm or kingdom," and we notice this happening from a very early age.

Life is all about fun for our boys during the Page stage. Fun is important for their development; it's not just a lighthearted pursuit. They're not yet thinking about training, practicing, or being able to improve at something for the future. For them, that's not really *worth it* because they don't see the value in anything that's not fun.

Everything is about the present moment for them and what's happening *right now*. If our Page is not very good at Little League, and he's not having fun at it, he'll say, "I don't want to play baseball."

He doesn't see the value of practicing to get better and thinks to himself, "Nope, I'm not good at this; I'm not having any fun, so I'm not going to play!"

Because this stage is all about adventure and challenging themselves, they'll be thinking "Can I lift this big rock? Can I catch that frog? How many steps can I jump down from?" They're always testing their abilities and asking themselves "Am I good at this? What can I do now?"

Pages and the Present

As mentioned, Pages are so deeply *present* in the moment that they aren't considering the benefit of learning or training for the future. The way they relate to themselves is tied to the moment they find themselves in, like, "This is who I am. This is how it is."

You'll be able to see what the Pages don't yet see. You can see the future possibilities and the impact that practice and learning will have on them. They're so busy enjoying the moment that the future isn't even a thought for them. That will change as they cross into Knighthood, but for now, they're all about the love of adventure.

Just imagine watching a Page — a little two-year-old boy walking around, exploring the environment and thinking "Can I lift those heavy books? Can I roll that big rock?" They're giving themselves challenges like "How fast can I run?" They are always testing themselves to ask how good they are at something and how they can "win" at it.

Think about it as the "adventure-testing" stage. Their Worth-It Calculation consists of these tests: "Is this fun? What will I get from this? Will I be able to succeed at this skill?"

Pages and Competition

Competition is also something that is innate in most men, and they experience it much differently than most women do. In my Masterclass Series 2-3, we explore what competition provides for men and how it is often viewed by most women. I've had the pleasure of spending time with two young Pages who are brothers. Mikie is five and Jimmy is three, and *everything* is a competition!

Mikie often races ahead of his slower little brother, exclaiming "I got there first!" or "I won! I was faster!" Mikie can jump farther, put his shoes on quicker, ride his scooter faster; the list goes on and on.

I sometimes caught myself saying to him, "It's not a competition, Mikie!" However, I was wrong because everything actually *is* a competition for them at this age. I've told Mikie that he might not always be taller or faster than Jimmy, but he doesn't believe me. In his view, he's older, so that means he will always be faster, stronger, smarter, taller, you name it! Because remember, it's all about the present moment for our little Pages.

Some questions we can ask a Page include the following:

What are you doing for fun?
What have you accomplished lately?
How have you been challenging yourself?

What Does a Page Need?

Pages need freedom, above all, to try out these new and challenging things. Holding them back upsets them and usually thrusts them into rebellion anyway. We can ease up a little on the protective stance and allow them to explore new things. When they do make choices that don't have a great outcome, compassion is needed. They're not thinking about the future; they're simply absorbed in the challenge of the moment.

Giving Pages the freedom to explore adventures and take on new things is essential. We can consciously let go instead of being nervous about them climbing high on the monkey bars, jumping down three steps at a time, or enjoying some other wild daredevil feat.

Of course, we're afraid that they'll get hurt (and to be honest, that fear rarely goes away, even as our children grow into adulthood). However, our little Pages need the freedom to explore these things in order to test themselves, learn, and grow. John, a man in the King stage of his life, had this to say about it:

> **Pages need freedom, above all, to try out these new and challenging things. Holding them back upsets them and usually thrusts them into rebellion anyway.**
> **We can ease up a little on the protective stance and allow them to explore new things.**
>
> BARBARA COLE SALMERON

I don't know that we ever completely outgrow the idea of testing ourselves. How is a man supposed to know what his strength is if it doesn't push him to the edge of the envelope? Where do you even know where the edge is if you haven't been there? I think it happens at all stages. That's certainly a driving force for the Page and the Prince in overcoming challenges. It is an essential element for the Knight, but I don't know if we completely outgrow it; I think it takes different forms. I think that we still put challenges in front of ourselves. I think that is one of the fundamental aspects that cause men to feel that what they do is worthwhile, that what they do matters. And I think that feeling as though we matter is hugely important not only to men, but to women as well.

When Pages "Fail"

The best thing we can do when a Page "fails" is to *validate* their experience: "Oh my gosh, I'm sorry that it didn't work." Then we can ask something like "Do you need anything from me?" or "What do you think you need to do now?"

Beyond that, we should *not* tell them or show them how to do it. Instead, we can just let them figure it out so they can experience that internal satisfaction of their external achievement. We'll hear them exclaim, "I did it!" And truly, it is the cutest thing ever! We will empower them by giving them opportunities to test themselves and be our hero as we watch their self-esteem grow — so just sit back, relax, and see your Page's development unfold before your very eyes.

You'll see me share this throughout the book — in every stage, men need appreciation. For a Page, that means expressing appreciation for what they *did* do: "You helped me bring in the groceries. Thank you so much; that's such a big help!" We can find tasks where they can help us, and we can let them be our heroes in creative ways. Of course, they won't do it as quickly or as neatly as we would have, and yet, that's perfectly fine! Trying new things, failing, and succeeding are all part of the learning cycle at any age, especially for a Page.

Pages and Video Games

A hugely misunderstood phenomenon with Pages is understanding why they are so obsessed with video games. Moms might see them playing and genuinely be baffled at what the point is.

The truth is video games are completely instinctual; they touch on the instincts of the hunter because it's all about getting points, conquering challenges, growing skills, and winning. These are all things that help Pages to feel like men! Carter, a married man who is now retired from the military shared, "Now that I'm in my 40's, I can't compete physically like I used to. Video games provide a form of competition, focus, camaraderie, achievement, and skill advancement to help keep me mentally sharp and growing."

Getting to reset the game over and over and advance to new levels is deeply fulfilling for any hunter, especially a Page. It is a testing ground for their abilities.

Now, I'm not saying to let them play for hours on end and not limit the amount of time they spend playing video games. It's good to set healthy boundaries, of course. What I am saying is that it's helpful to look at it through a different lens — it's a primal, instinctual thing that they're experiencing when playing video games. It's a place for them to challenge themselves, test their skills, and gain confidence while doing something fun.

Can you see how homework fits into the picture here? It's no fun, they don't win at it instantly, and they just usually won't see the point. We know that the point of homework is much greater than the actual assignment — it's about long-term learning. For a Page, however, they won't see this because they are so present-focused.

How can we make homework something fun for them? Sometimes, sitting and doing homework *with* them will feel like quality time to them. Think of how you can "gamify" homework, such as by setting a timer to see how much they can get done correctly before the timer goes off! You can also do some of the home-work with them and intentionally get your answers wrong and let them correct you. Compliment them on a job well done, and tell them they are very smart and learning faster than ever! Show them with your facial expressions and body language how impressed you are, and acknowledge their good efforts. This will also help build their self-esteem at this crucial age.

I know it can be tempting to "bribe" them to do their home-work with some kind of reward when they are done; however, most parenting experts agree that this is not a good idea. This reinforces the feeling that homework is drudgery and something to be suffered through to get the reward. It can also encourage a child to do the bare minimum to receive the reward and help them develop a sense of entitlement. Last, it can prevent them from developing an intrinsic motivation for learning, which can ultimately lead to a poor work ethic later in life. Instead, give your Page what he likely craves — *you!* Your time, attention, and admiration for a job well done can be very motivating at a young age. Always remember, fun is the name of the game with our little men!

An Interview with a Page

I was able to interview a Page, a four-year-old named Jesse. Here's how our interview went:
Me: "What are your favorite things to do?"
Jesse: "I like to play with trains and trucks."
Me: "Why?"
Jesse: "Because it's fun."
Me: "If you could do one thing all day, what would that be?"
Jesse: "Playing outside!"
Me: "Why?"
Jesse: "Because it's fun!"

At some point, I stopped asking the "why" question because every answer continued to be "because it's fun." Remember, *fun* is the primary focus of the Page!

Then I asked him, "What do you like to do outside?"

Jesse: "I play games, and I like going to the carnival. I like to play the games there."

Me: "What games do you like to play at the carnival?"

Jesse: "All of them!"

Me: "What would be your favorite prize to win?"

Jesse: "All of them!"

Later in the interview, I asked him about helping his dad at the auto repair shop.

Me: "Tell me about when you help your dad fix cars. What part do you do?"

Jesse: "My dad takes the tires off because the bolts are rusty. When it rains and snows, they get rusty. I get to put the new ones on. He doesn't like broken cars, and that's why he fixes them. And then people can go off again!"

Me: "What is the best part of doing that?"

Jesse: "Helping people out!"

Me: "How do you feel when you get to help people?"

Jesse: Looks at a feelings chart and points to *happy, excited, proud,* and *helpful.*

He was very proud and happy to be able to help his dad and help people with their cars. He became their little hero!

Even in this short interview with Jesse the Page, I could tell that it was very important to him to give me the *right and correct* answers ... translation: he was already striving to *provide* something for me at just four years old!

The Worth-It Calculation for a Page

What does the Worth-It Calculation look like for our little men in the Page stage?

Their internal calculation will sound something like this: "Is this a challenge? Is this fun? Will I be able to do this? And what will I get from it?"

With our men at any stage, if it doesn't pass his Worth-It Calculation, he won't be interested in doing it and will move on to something else.

> The internal Worth-It Calculation of a Page will sound something like this:
>
> "Is this a challenge?
> Is this fun?
> Will I be able to do this?
> What will I get from it?"
>
> BARBARA COLE SALMERON

If you don't remember the importance of the Worth-It Calculation, please revisit Chapter 3. I asked Rob, a business owner in the King stage, what his son's top priorities were (what is worth it) when he was in the Page stage, and he shared, "The most important things for him were playing with his friends and playing video games. He also told me it was very important for him to please his sister. He's someone who needs to feel connected. He needs to feel love, just like all of us do."

The Stages of Development in Cookie Form — Pages

I've created a cookie metaphor to help us understand the stages of development for our yummy, sweet, and sometimes crunchy men!

If a Page were a **cookie**, what kind of cookie would he be? His answer, of course, would be "All of them!"

He's not deciding anything yet. He's not molding himself into what he's going to be for the rest of his life. There are so many good choices and different cookie varieties, and he wants to taste them all!

At the Page stage, no future decisions have been made just yet. One day, he will say he wants to be a police officer; the next day, an astronaut; and the next week, a doctor. Can you see these characteristics in the little men you've known?

As we explore the next stages, here's *a word of warning:* If you want to talk to a man about the stages of development, I recommend that you first describe a little of each stage to him, or have him read this part of the book or the synopsis at the end of Chapter 8, or even watch my Masterclass 2–1. Then, ask him what stage *he* identifies with or what stage *he* thinks he's in.

Remember to *ask* a man what stage he is in; never *tell* him his stage! Of course, we're going to have our thoughts and our opinions about it. However, if we can ask questions and stay curious, we will discover new things about him in relation to the stages of development. By asking and listening, we will better understand what is important to him *now* and how we can best support him. This will usually spark extra motivation for him to provide for our needs, which is instinctual for him anyway. I've learned *the hard way* that criticizing, nagging, or otherwise belittling men usually gets the *opposite* of what we really want, as they withdraw and shut down.

Knight

The Knight stage typically begins after puberty. It might coincide with a little bit of middle school, definitely high school, and will continue into college. For some men, it could be all of college (and maybe even beyond). Most of them have not settled down into marriage just yet. There are a few exceptions, yet most are not ready to settle down at this stage because they're still exploring the world.

Again, our wonderful men are going to transition through these stages at different times, which is why I did not put specific age ranges in here. Their development will happen with fluidity depending on their life experiences and when their focus changes from what *used to be* important to what is *now* important to them.

This stage is quite similar to that of Pages, with a few distinctions. The Knight's focus is *also* adventure, testing, and fun, yet with a bit more focus on the future. He is moving out of the pure "present focus" of the Page. He starts to see the value of practicing to get good at something. Practicing his free throws can help the Knight become the MVP of his team or can help his team win the championship. See how important and *instinctual* competition and winning are to men?

Knights are still all about testing themselves in the world, *and* they begin to have an appreciation for training and skill building. They also demonstrate loyalty, and their life is all about *the pack* (their group of friends). I asked Carl, a business owner in the King stage, what stage he sees his son in currently, and he said, "I would say he's in the Knight stage. He's formed a brotherhood, so to speak. He's in college, and he's got a lot of great friends. He's started a fraternity, and he's in a house with several other guys. So, he's definitely living that Knight lifestyle."

Since Knights are still so invested in fun and adventure, most of us women have had our hearts broken by one. It often goes something like this:

Knight: "It's really fun being with you."
Woman: "Yes, this is so much fun. Do you want to stay together forever?"
Knight: "What? We're just having fun!"

A Knight may be in a relationship; however, that doesn't mean he is ready to settle down just yet! He is still learning about himself and the world around him, and *most* Knights are not yet making lifelong decisions. There are always exceptions, of course. Some young men feel compelled to build their kingdom first and then find their queen. Others commit to a relationship early and want to build the kingdom together with their significant other. Can you think of an example of each scenario you've seen with the men in your life?

What Does a Knight Need?

Knights need that freedom of feeling like we're not dictating what they should do. When we tell them how something is or how to do something, they will likely limit their communication with us. They need to discover the world for themselves. Anyone who has raised teenagers will know *exactly* what I mean!

Another big part of Knighthood is needing respect *for their friends*. We can witness them entering this stage when suddenly, life becomes all about being with their friends. If we happen to say anything bad about their friends, question the quality of their friends, or even make negative comments about how much time they spend with them, they'll choose to stop talking to us about them.

So, to maintain connection and harmony with your Knight, find some things that you appreciate about *the pack*. Look for some good things to point out about his friends. If we can do this, he will be more open to keeping us in the conversation when it comes to this part of his life.

I had a research interview with Andre, an eighteen-year-old male college student in the Knight stage, and asked him, "What are the struggles for you and your friends in college?" He said the following:

> There's a lot of pressure on us that stems directly from relationships and finding a girlfriend, and honestly, from losing your virginity. Especially at such a young age, there's a lot of pressure. When being in a group, there's this idea of trying to prove oneself as the alpha male; the position of a beta male is never socially acceptable. There's always this constant underlying fight toward being the alpha male, and then also the fight toward obtaining sexual experiences if one has not had that at all, and there's so much pressure from society.

Now, that is straight from the mouth of a Knight! Our conversation continued, as I found it fascinating to learn about Knights from a young man who said he was in the middle of that stage. Please keep an open and curious mind as you read about his perspective.

Me: "How is one crowned the alpha male in those groups?"

Andre: "One way is how much one drinks compared to others. If one drank the most, one would completely achieve the whole position of alpha male. Also, the sexual experiences for alpha males, because if one achieves the position of the alpha male, then they're automatically assumed and given all these privileges, something not received by someone who isn't the alpha male."

Me: "Aside from those benefits, why is becoming the alpha male of the group important?"

Andre: "Oh, it's everything! Recognition is probably one of the most desired concepts for young men. And while one strives to become the alpha male, they lose so many natural characteristics of themselves, which is so frustrating. The most frustrating part about it is that almost everyone gets caught up in it, whether they want to or not."

Me: "And then what happens?"

Andre: "Once you achieve that position, you inherit everything, like social recognition, friends, and sexual experiences. The reason this goes so hand in hand is because with obtaining sexual experiences, you become the alpha male, and that's what so many conversations revolve around, especially in college."

Me: "What if someone doesn't play along?"

Andre: "It's not rewarded in our culture to be an outcast or not fit in with the pack."

As you can see, in the Knight stage, young men also need the freedom to explore new things and take risks (just like Pages). Like every other stage, Knights need appreciation for what they're doing for us or in the world. We can also give them opportunities to be our heroes because they need to be needed.

They need admiration for their effort, for their good attempt at something. So don't be afraid to use positive reinforcement to express how much you admire what they've done. Even if they fall short, rather than correct them (which 99 percent of the time *will* be received as criticism), we want to empower them by putting it back on them. We can do that by asking a Knight "What do *you* think you need?" rather than telling them what *we think* they need.

This stage is really all about them exploring and learning. The Knights are out there having fun on their adventures. In my interview with Mary, a college student, she said, "I see my brother as someone who is very mature, but he's very quick to anger. I feel like he's more in the Knight stage just because he is incapable of handling his emotions and reactions. He definitely is not in the Prince stage yet, where he could effectively build professional connections, because he needs to know how to be OK with himself first."

With Knights, we can also begin to interact with them about the concept of honor, which naturally starts to form for them. We can converse with them about being a good man, making good choices, and doing the right thing. Knights are focused on developing and testing their skills and character, often comparing themselves to a role model they respect or admire, such as a respected grandfather or some public figure.

> With Knights, we can also begin to interact with them about the concept of honor, which naturally starts to form for them.
>
> We can converse with them about being a good man, making good choices, and doing the right thing.
>
> — BARBARA COLE SALMERON

Something I want to acknowledge about Knights is that they are always struggling with *the right thing versus* the *fun thing*. Sometimes, just recognizing that they're wrestling with this choice can be really valuable. Validation goes a long way for every person, no matter their stage or gender. Most of us want to be seen, heard, and understood, right? Positive acknowledgment of their choices helps them to feel seen and respected, and we know how important respect is to our men!

> No person was ever honored for what he received.
>
> Honor has been the reward for what he gave.
>
> — CALVIN COOLIDGE

For example, say a Knight wants to go out with their friends, and maybe they have a younger sibling who needs help with something. Their parents can acknowledge the difficult choice by saying, "One thing is the fun thing to do, and this other thing might be the right thing to do, so let's have a conversation about it and see what it *provides* for others." This way of responding to their situation gives them the opportunity to be a hero because they now understand the concept of honor.

Knights in the Workplace

Our Knights seek out challenges because they gather a sense of growth and fulfillment by completing them. In working with Knights, I find they need a variety of new challenges and training, and we can give that to them in the workplace. They need ways to increase their skills in a manner where they feel like they have autonomy over their learning.

We should do our best to refrain from dictating exactly *what* they should do and *how* they should do it. As a Knight, they need the freedom to pursue a variety of paths. We can say things like "Well, you might consider this," or we could ask, "What do you think about looking at it from this angle?" Jack, a scientist in the King stage, shared his thoughts on this with me:

I've always been adventurous because that's the nature of the career I was in. It's not that much different now; it's just a continuation. I mean, in some sense, I've always been a Knight, you could say. Every few years, I would do something different, something significant. That's still what I'm doing now. It's just now I'm doing it within my own company and I wouldn't want it any other way.

Make sure any ideas you share with a Knight sound like a *suggestion* rather than a demand because, again, they can stop communicating with us if we attempt to tell them what's "true" and what's not.

The Worth-It Calculation for a Knight

For a Knight, his Worth-It Calculation is all about "What am I learning? What are my adventures? And what are the challenges to help me advance or level up?"

One of the things that we see a lot is when a Knight is very good at something, yet it might *not* be challenging for them. People can tell them that they are so great at music and they should definitely be a musician. However, it may or may not be challenging enough for them. So, for the Knight, they're going to look for what they're good at and ask "What is this testing or challenging in me? What new skills will I get? Is this worth it?"

> For a Knight, his Worth-It Calculation is all about:
>
> "What am I learning? What are my adventures? What are the challenges to help me advance or level up?"
>
> BARBARA COLE SALMERON

I asked Rob, a father of two who is in the King stage, about his college-age son, and he shared, "I think he is a Knight because he is a mix of instant gratification now and somewhat thinking about his future too. He has short-term goals, and two years is a long-term goal with him right now. What's he going to do beyond two years? He doesn't know. He only knows that he has his education goals and staying happy with his girlfriend."

The Stages of Development in Cookie Form — Knights

So, if the Knight were a cookie, what kind of cookie would he be? Let's say he's decided that his flavor in life is chocolate. He's a chocolate cookie, and yet, how many different variations of chocolate cookies are out there? He hasn't narrowed it down to just one yet. He's going to explore them all!

Something to Know About the Knight Stage

One thing I want to mention here is that *most men are always some part Knight!* They almost always have that Knight stage in them and that flair for needing to have fun, adventure, and challenges throughout their entire lifetime.

Adventure can take on many different flavors; what "adventure" means to a man changes over the course of his life and is always going to be different from man to man. Some men are going to be into skydiving, scuba diving, or exotic travel. For others, their adventure will be more intellectual, like learning a new language or advanced skill or earning another degree. A promotion or a new, challenging project at work can also be considered an adventure for some men. Ladies, can you see the importance of allowing space for the men in your life to experience various adventures? Steer clear of dimming his light when it comes to having fun, and watch how lit up the men in your life become.

I interviewed John, a consultant in the King stage, and asked him about adventure. He shared, "I don't know that I can ever make the claim that I have divorced myself from the appeal of an adventure."

Prince

The Prince stage is when our men turn their attention to building their kingdom. It's something that they are very serious about and where much of their energy, resources, and attention are spent. They are *compelled by instinct* to build! Remember that being compelled by instinct feels like being forced or driven by an overpowering, irresistible internal urge. It's not logic; it's instinct! This could be expressed as building a career, a family, or something within their communities like a non-profit or a church.

There are three sub-stages of the Prince stage: Early, Middle, and Late. The Prince stage can begin when a man is in his early thirties, although it could start earlier or later into his forties. As always, it's different for each man.

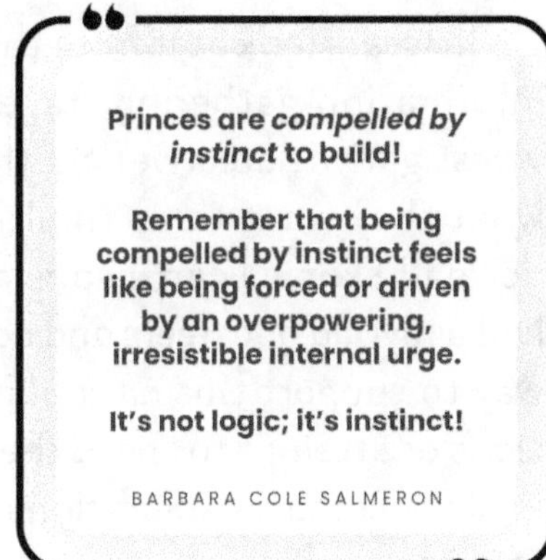

Early Prince

The Early Prince is concerned with the question of *what* and *where* they will build. They're in the exploration stage to get a sense of how they want their kingdom to look. They are fresh out of the Knight stage, so they still have a strong focus on adventure.

As they explore what fits for them, they go 100 percent all in as they explore one path at a time. The fact that they switch from one interest or career path to another may be jarring for those *witnessing* the indecision of Early Princes; however, it's important to let them do this! It is completely normal for them to change majors in college or even change careers in the Early Prince stage.

They're a little unsure about where they want to focus their energy in their build. Changing their mind and wrestling with important decisions are common in this stage. For example, they may be studying something in one area (building their skills) and then abruptly switch their focus to another — just as I switched from Pre-Med to Business in college!

With an Early Prince, we can watch how excited and inter-ested they are in different things. It's all explorative. For someone not viewing men through this particular lens, it can seem that they're indecisive and "don't know where they are going in life."

Instead, look at it from the vantage point of the necessary information-gathering stage the men are in (they're like an investigative detective). So, they may change their mind about what they want to do (multiple times), which is completely normal! I know I can also relate to this in my own life, having had a myriad of careers and adventures over the years. The best way to support this *natural process* is to not force their decisions or attempt to speed them up. Supporting an Early Prince in his necessary explorations is a very loving and compassionate response.

What Does an Early Prince Need?

The best way to support an Early Prince is to understand their explorative behavior (hopefully, by reading this book, you already see more about where they are). From that point of view, we can give them the space to explore without making them "wrong" or negatively judging them when they change their minds. When we don't expect them to pick something and stick with it, they can feel *free and supported* to make their own decisions.

A caveat here that's helpful to remember is that in these modern times, young people have more options available to them to change their minds when it comes to their studies and work. The previous generations who were raising Early Princes might say, "In my day, we chose a job and stuck with it our entire lives."

> The best way to support an Early Prince is to understand their explorative behavior.
>
> From that point of view, we can give them the space to explore without making them "wrong" or negatively judging them when they change their minds.
>
> BARBARA COLE SALMERON

For those generations, especially in certain cultures and socio-economic conditions, they simply didn't have the option to be as explorative as they desired to be when they were in their Early Prince stage.

Nowadays, it's normal. In fact, the National Center for Education Statistics reports that 80 percent of college students will change their major at least once, with the current norm being about three times during their time in college.[7] That was certainly true in my case! What about you?

Let's celebrate our Early Princes by giving them this freedom and letting them really take advantage of that desire to explore themselves fully in this stage of life.

An Early Prince in the Workplace

In their professional endeavors, Early Princes need to see that what they are doing in the workplace has some kind of path to a specific future they desire. Otherwise, they'll do the bare minimum or find a way out toward a new venture that feels like a better fit.

If we have an Early Prince working for or with us, it can be very helpful to directly ask them, "How do you see working at this company as a path to your future?" If their role isn't really leading directly to a career path, we can still ask them a similar question such as "What do you feel you will gain out of this experience?" This question helps them to reflect on what the experience can provide for them or how it can help them build upon their next steps — like gaining skills, connections, or knowledge.

---

7 "Normalizing the Norm of Changing College Majors," November 5, 2020. University of Tulsa (Online resource)

The Worth-It Calculation for an Early Prince

For the Early Prince, the centerpiece of his Worth-It Calculation is all about what he is interested in building. For example, if he's about to go to college and is asking himself *what* will make these four years *worth it*.

Or, if they're still in high school and already drifting into the Early Prince stage, they might say, "What will make these four years in high school worth it — worth my time and my effort?" These students will really focus more intently on certain areas of development, such as sports or academics, with their future college and career paths in mind.

> **For the Early Prince, the centerpiece of his Worth-It Calculation is all about what he is interested in building.**
>
> **For example, if he's about to go to college, he's asking himself what will make these four years *worth it*.**
>
> BARBARA COLE SALMERON

At first, most Early Princes are going to do this, and then they'll switch to doing that, and then maybe even go back to this again. It'll be a lot of trying things on and wearing different hats, so to speak. What's important for us to remember as we witness all this switching back and forth is that internally, they are always asking themselves "What is worth doing? What am I interested in building? What stimulates my thinking?"

Keep in mind, these are very *normal* scenarios for Early Princes:

- Changing their majors or degrees in college
- Being indecisive about a career path
- Starting a new job, and a few months in, realizing they don't want to do that job anymore
- Going to college out of state, only to return home after a semester or two

The Stages of Development in Cookie Form — Early Princes

If an Early Prince were a cookie, what kind of cookie would he be? He'd be cookie dough. Yes, there are many different flavors of cookie dough, and he's still figuring out which dough he would be — the decision hasn't been made yet, so he hasn't started the baking process.

In his excitement and interest in many different things, he finds delight; it's delicious for him to be the dough right now! Later, he will decide the flavor (his future path), and in the next few stages, that really starts to happen!

A Little Story ...

I was interviewing Carl — a man in his early fifties, and he shared that his girlfriend, Simone, was concerned that her son was going to be stuck in the Knight stage forever! But what Carl described sounded more like an Early Prince. He said this about the young man: "He's asked his girlfriend to marry him. Now, he's actually doing some planning. He's thinking of going back to school because, for him, now, that's all worth it. It's worth it for him to go to school, and it's worth it for him to get trained because he wants to build this future with this fiancée." Can you see how he is deciding where and how to build his kingdom?

When I shared with Carl the differences between the Knight stage and Prince stage and posed the question of how his girl-friend's son may already be transitioning to Prince, he got it. The fact that he committed to two big areas of his life to build — career and relationship — clearly shows that he has already entered the building stage of the Prince. Carl shared this with Simone, and the worried mom began to relax with more peace of mind that she could now watch her son develop in his own way.

Additionally, when I interviewed Mary, a female college student, she said the following about her boyfriend: "My boyfriend is twenty, but he has different priorities. He thinks in terms of career-oriented and family-oriented goals. He's always trying to contribute to his family, and he thinks of how he can develop himself professionally, in school and in work. He also manages the finances of his dad's business."

Here we see in both examples people who, even though they are in their early twenties, are both showing signs of being Early Princes. Remember, it can happen at all different ages. These are some examples of earlier transitions.

Middle Prince

The transition from Early to Middle Prince is subtle, yet one worth mentioning. Once you see the Middle Prince stage, you likely won't be able to *unsee* it!

The Middle Prince is now much more focused on build-ing, building, building, and working all of the time — he's a workhorse who is barely coming up for air! At this stage, it's very normal for him to hardly ever see his spouse or romantic partner, as his *instinctual* urge is to build, rather than focus on connec-tion. This can cause some issues within relationships, especially when the partner doesn't understand that he is in this Middle Prince stage and is *compelled by instinct* to build, build, build!

> The Middle Prince is now much more focused on building, building, building, and working all of the time — he's a workhorse who is barely coming up for air!
>
> At this stage, it's very normal for him to hardly ever see his spouse or romantic partner, as his *instinctual* urge is to build, rather than focus on connection.
>
> BARBARA COLE SALMERON

What Does a Middle Prince Need?

They need a lot of support from us to acknowledge their progress and achievements. They are already *highly aware* of what they *don't yet* have and where they're *not yet* winning. Being reminded of their actual progress makes it "worth it" for them. We can point out their wins at work, for example, and validate their hard work and long hours. Celebrate any promotions, raises, goals reached, and new accounts or clients. Any accomplishment is worth celebrating! They begin to feel victorious, and it fuels them and motivates their efforts to keep moving forward. Even sex can be supportive validation for a Middle Prince!

Carter, who is retired from the military and now in his second career, expressed it this way: "It's hard for me to acknowledge that. Why do I have to feel 'worth it' from other people's responses or feedback? But I do find satisfaction from the feedback of others when I do good things or when I perform at a level where they can say 'Thanks, man, you did a good job.'" Carter is self-aware enough to know that he shouldn't need feedback from others, and he's honest enough to admit that it does feel like support and encouragement for him.

If there's a significant other in a Middle Prince's life, that person can often feel very neglected during this time. However, pointing this out to the Middle Prince will only backfire. It will continue to feed the insecurities he already has around how he's not "winning." It also definitely won't get the significant other the result they are seeking, such as more connection and more time with him. Quite the opposite; he will often withdraw because requesting more of his attention is usually perceived as criticism. I really learned this one the hard way through *lots* of trial and error! Even when we don't mean it as criticism, it's hard for our Middle Princes to *not* receive it that way.

When (and if) he does have time to come up for air and go on a date with us or spend time with the kids, we need to treat his time as if it's on a really tight budget — because it is.

We can risk *blowing the budget* by spending our time together complaining about how small the budget is. And guess what? That just makes it even smaller! I invite you to treat his time as very precious. We don't want to waste the small amount of time we have with him by complaining and still not getting the result we wanted. We want to make the most of the time we have with him, so plan a nice date, pay him compliments, and have fun with him. And I know how cliché this sounds; however, cook his favorite meal for him or grab his favorite takeout! The old adage "The way to a man's heart is through his stomach" is true! And, I would argue, the other path to a man's heart is in the bedroom! Remember, because of men's much higher testosterone levels, sex is usually more of a biological *need* than it is for most women. However, the intimacy in our love life can also help women to feel the connection we yearn for.

I don't want to turn you into a 1930s housewife, I promise! I'm just illustrating that when a man is in this particular stage, his instinct to provide is on overdrive as he is building his kingdom. There is very little balance. I want you to get the best result in connecting with him! Remember, this work is based on over three decades of research with tens of thousands of men and women. If you are in a relationship with a Middle Prince and not getting the result you want, experiment with some of these suggestions and see if they help!

I recognize that this is a difficult time in a relationship for his significant other. During the Middle Prince stage, I recommend his romantic partner have their own activities to focus on in their life, to find activities that fill their tank and other interests that fulfill them. Know that it won't always be like this! In his mind, he knows he is also doing this *for* you and the family. He is building the kingdom for all of you! This is why it can be so frustrating *for him* when we don't see that.

I asked Tom, a married man in the King stage in his fifties, how his wife supported him through that stage. And he said, "By not nagging me. She was very good at knowing that my career was very important to me and that I had a job with very long days. I was never that guy who got the phone call saying 'You always work; that's all you do.' I never got the nag. My wife has a life. I have a life. Together, we have a life. It's just the way we built it." I asked Tom if his wife ever complained to him about his long days at work, and he shared, "No. We have a great marriage. She helped me when I had my business, and then she went back to work. We do a lot of stuff in our marriage; it's called interdependent versus codependent."

> I recognize that this is a difficult time in a relationship for his significant other.
>
> During the Middle Prince stage, I recommend his romantic partner have their own activities to focus on in their life, to find activities that fill their tank and other interests that fulfill them.
>
> BARBARA COLE SALMERON

Remember, there is very little balance in the Middle Prince stage! Carter, a man in the Tunnel (another stage we will discuss shortly), summed it up this way: "There's a level of progression where you could be really good at your job, really good at fixing things, but if you couldn't teach others to fix things, or can't teach others to be like you, you would be moved out. That is where I saw the development of young men moving from Knight to Prince. Most of the men that I've met and mentored were Princes building to the detriment of a bunch of other stuff." Ladies, I know this lack of balance can feel really sucky. Most of us have been there! It can feel like his compulsion to build will last forever, but eventually, there will be more balance. Keep reading!

The Worth-It Calculation for a Middle Prince

So, what makes something worth it for the Middle Prince? He needs to see and feel the victories in what he is doing, along with his wins and accomplishments. He needs to see the progress that he's making in exchange for his efforts. Jack, a consultant and King in his fifties, had this to share: "Most people in my field are Princes in some respect because either they're trying to climb a managerial ladder or working at a company where they're trying to make something big happen." Seeing his own progress helps make the Middle Prince's efforts to be *worth it*.

A Middle Prince will ask himself, "Does this job, degree, or relationship contribute to what I'm building? Will this be something that's worth learning for my future?" And, of course, he'll ask, "Is this fun to build?" Remember, all that building is typically associated with career and finances; however, it can also be focused on family or community. I asked Carl where he sees examples of men in the Prince stage in his life, and he shared, "I do belong to an all men's Toastmasters group. The young guys there are in their mid-twenties and are definitely in the Prince stage. That's why they're at Toastmasters — they're building a future, and they want to become really good public speakers and be influential in their business." Carl also shared this about his own experience: "I identify with more of a Middle or Late Prince, even though I'm fifty-one now, and I should be in the King stage. I put myself on the back burner to take care of my family and later ended

> **The Worth-It Calculation for a Middle Prince:**
>
> **He needs to see and feel the victories in what he is doing, along with his wins and accomplishments. He needs to see the progress that he's making in exchange for his efforts.**
>
> BARBARA COLE SALMERON

up getting divorced. I was about forty-five by the time I started working on my career and building my kingdom."

Kevin, a married gay man who is in a *state* we call Elder, had this to say about his experience in the Prince stage:

I would say building, building, building my family was my focus once Ed and I got together. You couldn't build a family and a career on the same track. Eddie and I were both captains in the Air Force, and we were living over-seas. We knew that it was time for us to come back to the United States, but at that time, if we wanted to stay together, one of us had to get out. It was not possi-ble for both of us to continue our military careers and stay together. When we got to Dallas, I started building again. I was actually fired for being gay from that job. So I had to build again. But yeah, I still have some build-ing in me today. I'm building my blog, and right now, I'm submerged in comedy.

The Middle Prince stage lasts anywhere from several years to over a decade, depending on the man's life experiences, as well as what he's chosen to build. In a rare example, a man I interviewed told me about a young coworker of his who was very serious about building at a young age. This young man was very focused on training to become a welder while still in high school. As soon as he graduated from high school, he went straight into welding with the goal of having his own business that would allow for a comfortable retirement. He is so young, and yet he's thinking so far ahead! He entered the Middle Prince stage early because he was clear on *what he wanted to build*. Can you see it?

The Stages of Development in Cookie Form — Middle Princes

What kind of cookie would our Middle Prince be? He has decided who he is; he is chocolate chip cookie dough. With that decision settled, his superpower of Single Focus turns to going from dough to cookie, completing the bake — that is, to *complete the building of his kingdom.*

When that Middle Prince is almost done with building his kingdom — when he's approaching his goal — he's *compelled* to push through to the finish line. This is when he moves into the Late Prince stage.

Late Prince

A Late Prince is *almost* done with his building, just not quite yet. He's experienced some accomplishments in building his kingdom and it's important that he's not distracted before he reaches the finish line. Yet, he will allow some breaks for fun, and other things will start to be important to him, like quality time with his partner and kids (if he has any). Hooray!

> A Late Prince is *almost* done with his building, just not quite yet.
>
> He's experienced some accomplishments in building his kingdom, and it's important that he's not distracted before he reaches the finish line.
>
> BARBARA COLE SALMERON

What Does a Late Prince Need?

The need for Late Princes to have validation and appreciation is even stronger than what the Early and Middle Princes need — it is paramount to them at this stage. Since the Late Prince is so close to his goal and doesn't want to be distracted before he reaches the finish line, showing our gratitude for his efforts and for the time he *can* spend with us will be very much appreciated!

Tom described his experience in the Late Prince stage in this way: "In 2001, my focus started turning to wanting to be able to enjoy what I do. And that's when I started working on not just building but pulling back and making sure that everything was taken care of so I could retire at fifty-five." Can you see what his finish line was?

If we are able to support Late Princes with attention, affection, sex, food, encouragement, and even a helping hand in more practical ways, he is more likely to value the relationship. It will genuinely be *worth it* for him to continue to be in the relationship *if* it is supporting his race to the finish line, which is his big life goals.

Not all Princes will be able to hold on to a relationship during their building stage. Remember, some Princes will want to build their kingdom with their significant other by their side. Other men will want to build their kingdom first and then go find their partner and move them in. Our amazing men have all sorts of internal beliefs about *how and when* they'll be ready for a committed relationship or fatherhood. Much of it is based on what they saw as examples when they were growing up, and it's a deeply fabulous conversation to have with them!

The Worth-It Calculation for a Late Prince

Since he is nearing the finish line and doesn't want any distractions to take him away from his goal, the Late Prince's Worth-It Calculation takes into account how much focus he can sustain. In regard to other activities or even a romantic relationship, he will be asking himself, "Will this distract me from what I'm building? Does this contribute to my overall goal? Is this helping me with what I have already started building?"

When it comes to a relationship or deepening a commitment to marriage, the Worth-It Calculation for a Late Prince has to do with how well the relationship is supporting him. A question we can ask ourselves to see how we may fit into this calculation is "Are he and his goals *at an advantage because of what I'm providing for him?*"

> **The Late Prince's Worth-It Calculation:**
>
> *"Will this distract me from what I'm building?*
> *Does this contribute to my overall goal?*
> *Is this helping me with what I have already started building?"*
>
> BARBARA COLE SALMERON

When it comes to their relationships, Late Princes will ask themselves, "Is this relationship encouraging, inspiring, and helping me reach my goal? Or is it hindering my efforts to reach my goal or the finish line?"

The Stages of Development in Cookie Form — Late Princes

At this stage, a Late Prince will feel that he can take a break for fun every now and then. Other things are starting to become important to him as he's slowing down and coming up for air. That's good news for his partner or family!

Still, that instinct to not be distracted before he crosses the finish line is so powerful! So, what kind of cookie is a Late Prince? He's still his particular flavor of cookie dough, as decided in the Middle Prince stage, and now he's about to go into the oven!

Which Prince Is He?

If you're considering which stage of Prince a man might be in, here's a helpful way to differentiate between the three.

Since the focus of all Princes is on building, they are in the Early Prince stage when they are considering *what* they are interested in building. They're still figuring out *where* to place their focus. You'll see that they may pick one college major or career path and then change their mind if they think it doesn't suit them. They're *eliminating* the directions as they decide against them. It is completely normal for an Early Prince to keep switching and searching!

The Middle Prince is concerned with whether what they are doing is *worthwhile* for their goals — especially when skill building or climbing the corporate ladder. They are *compelled* by instinct to build, build, build! They will rarely come up for air and are usually more focused on producing their desired result than they are on connection.

Finally, the Late Prince is focused on whether he will be distracted from *finishing* his goal or not. He will begin to be more open to fun and spending time with you, but he needs to be sure that what he's already built still gets enough of his attention and effort to cross the finish line. He will evaluate what and who in his life supports him in realizing his big goals, which are now so close he can taste them!

About All the Prince Stages

All three types of Princes will still have a very strong adventure element in how they do things and what they decide to do. Additionally, every Prince will really need that validation and appreciation while they are busily building (as well as in every other stage).

If we keep noticing what they've accomplished, pointing it out to them, and encouraging their efforts, we won't go wrong. Most men tend to be painfully aware of what they have *not yet accomplished*, so they definitely don't need us to wave around a flag of failure, pointing these things out to them. They see it already, Ladies! It's a big part of why they work so hard in the Prince stage.

We may think that we are helping by acknowledging what still needs to be completed; however, doing so will usually backfire and lead to him shutting down and not desiring the connection and quality time that we so dearly want with him.

The reason it leaves him frustrated is because part of *his protect and provide* instincts drive him to achieve these goals *for* the family or the relationship. In that way, he won't understand why his significant other doesn't *see* it and why they can only see what is, so far, "unfinished." This often is a big point of conflict for both people in the relationship. The partner asks why he is working so much, and he asks why they are unable to see he's doing it for both of them!

Ladies — I Hear You. What About Your Needs? Now, Hear Me Out ...

I know that many women reading this may be thinking that all of this support seems very one-sided. When I first started learning this, that thought definitely crossed my mind, too — a lot!

What about your needs? What about the time and connection that you need for the relationship to feel *worth it* for you? If a woman is feeling neglected, she might ask why she should be offering all this support without receiving what she wants in return.

I hear you, and I get it! I struggled with this a *lot* when I first learned about the male brain, *and* I was dating a Middle Prince at that time. I eventually chose to pursue my own interests and respect what he was building, which was, after all, for our future together. This choice gave me the freedom to pursue my own dreams, and as a small business owner, I needed all that extra time anyway to build my own Queendom.

The time and effort you will *invest* in working to fully understand men and adjusting your interactions and communication with them will help you get your needs met far *faster and more easily* than in the past. So hang in there because soon, you'll be fully equipped with more knowledge than any of your girlfriends! You'll notice some of these conflicts in *their* relationships, and once you see it, *you won't be able to unsee it.*

I've witnessed it time and time again: when we *give support and appreciation* to our men, it comes back to us tenfold in unexpected and delightful ways! Just trust that a deeper and more satisfying relationship with men is possible, and right now, you're learning the how-to. I promise it'll be worth it, and my journey (and the journeys of tens of thousands of others) is proof that these concepts can truly take us from hot mess to happily ever after!

> **The time and effort you will *invest* in working to fully understand men and adjusting your interactions and communication with them will help you get your needs met far *faster and more easily* than in the past.**
>
> BARBARA COLE SALMERON

Ladies, consider this scenario:

You are building a career or business you love, and you're feeling happy and fulfilled. You are crushing your goals and setting bigger ones each year. You're so close to that promotion or that huge client you've been working toward when, suddenly, your significant other gives you an ultimatum: dial back on the career or lose the relationship.

Hardly a fair choice, is it? No one likes to be backed into a corner and forced to choose. Now, we may think that we aren't asking our men to choose but look at any complaints about the relationship versus intentionally supporting his career. One has him feeling frustrated and criticized because we don't see that everything he does is also *for us.* The other has him feeling like you have his back; you are on his team and will be there for him. Which kind of support would *you* prefer?

If you were unwilling or unable to give up your career, what would you do? You might start to realize that even if you love your partner and want the relationship, you are simply unable to give up on everything you've been building.

Now, I can hear you thinking exactly what I used to think before learning about how different the male brain is from my own: *How about some balance? Surely, they can dial it back, right?* The reality is, in the Prince stage, there is very little balance. However, don't fear! There will be more capacity for a work-life balance once our men enter the King stage. Phew!

But first (coming up in the next chapter), let's explore the transitional *phase* between Prince and King: the Tunnel. You'll also uncover more revelations about the King stage and the state of Elder in the upcoming pages.

Page, Knight, and Prince — Self-Reflection Questions

- Have you known, or do you know, any little men who might be in the Page stage?
- Have you known, or do you know, any young men who might be in the Knight stage?
- Have you known, or do you know, any men who might be in the Early Prince stage?
- Have you known, or do you know, any men who might be in the Middle Prince stage?
- Have you known, or do you know, any men who might be in the Late Prince stage?

Eight

Men's Development— Later Stages

Now that you know all about the early, exploratory, and building stages of men's development, you'll enjoy learning more about the mature stages! Why? Because the men in these stages are grounded, wiser, and in harmony with their values. Doesn't that sound delicious? Keep reading; you are in the home stretch!

The Tunnel

There is a key *phase* between the Late Prince stage and the King stage: the Tunnel. Going back to the cookie analogy, *this is the oven* — and he is about to be baked! In this phase, our men are intensely questioning everything. They have achieved a level of success and start questioning what's *most* important in life.

Because everything is in question, they rarely fully commit to something. When they're in the Tunnel, our men will ask themselves questions about all parts of their lives, what they're doing, and especially what they stand for.

I interviewed Carter, a married father of two in his mid-forties, and when I told him about the Tunnel, he said, "I'm definitely in that place now. I reflect, *Where have I gone wrong?* Even professionally, relationally with my wife, and even religiously. I'm at a stage right now where I'm doing a lot of work to understand my religious culture and my life psychologically, emotionally, spiritually, relationally. So, I'm doing a lot of digging on many foundational things. Does that put me in the Tunnel?"

Being in the Tunnel is like one giant Worth-It Calculation. Everything becomes about the following questions: *What is worth it? What do I really care about? What's most important in my life?* Carter also shared, "There's that phrase 'a period of intense questioning.' Yeah, I'm definitely in that stage now. There's a discomfort at this stage between my wife and me. I don't know how to articulate this as well. Why am I questioning so much? I mean, like, a ton."

Often, something very serious can happen in a man's life, and that will pull him into the Tunnel — this could be a divorce, the death of a loved one, or a serious illness for him or someone close to him. These experiences make all of us reflect on what is most important.

A man in the Tunnel will re-evaluate what is in alignment with his values and how he is spending his resources (money, energy, and time) while still on this earth. This period of intense questioning and introspection can be very uncomfortable for him and can be viewed as a "midlife crisis" by society. It's not really a crisis, although it can certainly feel like one for him and for you! Rob, a King and father of two, had this experience:

> The Tunnel was when I got divorced. I never found myself questioning my life or what the meaning of it should be. The only thing I questioned was marriage. I thought marriage was bullshit. That's the Tunnel I've been through, and at that time, my conclusion was, "I'm not going to be falling in love again." That was an example of the Worth-It Calculation. Is this what the benefit is? It's not worth it; I'm done with this shit. When I went through that time, it was a very toxic period in my life.

Many men won't experience something so serious when they enter the Tunnel. This stage could simply mean that they've achieved their goals — they've got the income, house, car, and even family (all the things we *think* will bring happiness and satisfaction), and there's a "now what?" moment. They have all of these things that they worked so hard to achieve, and when they finally take a pause after so much building, they will question how they now want to spend their time. Where should they exert their precious energy? Their Worth-It Calculation begins to make a major shift. Tom, a married King, had this to say about his experience in the Tunnel:

The day I turned forty, I looked in the mirror, and in that moment, I knew that I knew shit, but I really didn't know. And the older I've gotten, the less I actually know. It's been a pretty cool place to come from because it's actually supported me in retiring at fifty-five. Because I previously thought I knew everything, and since I knew everything, I wasn't open to different ideas on how to invest money or how to do whatever. But truthfully, I didn't know shit. I was just at a different place. When I turned forty, it was an epiphany day.

The Tunnel, for some men, can be very short and barely noticeable. For others, it can be long, drawn out, and even painful. My mentor, colleagues, and I have seen, in our decades of research interviews with men, that they can spend up to three years in the Tunnel! One thing we've found that can help men in the Tunnel is doing some deep personal development work, such as seminars, workshops, and the like. This work can help them get clear on their values *much quicker* while also having other aha moments and breakthroughs *in a matter* of days rather than years!

I asked Kevin, a married Elder (Elder is the final state, described later in this chapter), if he remembers experiencing the Tunnel, and he shared,

I'd say it was at my last real job, the job that I retired from. I was in healthcare product sales, and I started having a real problem with what I did, which I hadn't had when I began. But I started thinking: *It's a shell game. All we're doing is moving money around. All the big money that I make is going right on the backs of the patient. You* don't want your customers to be well when you make more money off of illness. Morally, I think it is immoral for people to make a lot of money off of other people's illnesses. And I believe that strongly now.

You will learn how important men's personal values become to them when we discuss the King stage. For now, do you know some men in your life who have gone through the Tunnel?

What Do Men in the Tunnel Need?

When our men enter the Tunnel, they need respect for where they are. They need us to trust and honor the process of their intense life questioning.

Rather than getting anxious because of the internal considerations that they *might share* with you (most of this intense questioning is internal) or because of how you see them act, *listen* to them with curiosity. Do your best *not* to be attached to how it will affect the future, and you'll be able to be a sounding board and a place of calm for what can be a very anxious time for many men. Be present and know that this stage is temporary. Jack, a married King and father of two, described his Tunnel experience this way:

In 2011, after I had been working for the first company I'd ever worked at for almost seventeen years, I just came to the conclusion I didn't want to work there anymore. And that was a combination of how bureaucratic the company had become and my perception that I didn't really have a very attractive career future there at that point for a number of reasons. I was just turning fifty. So, I thought, *Well, if I want to make a switch out of*

> *this, I probably shouldn't wait too long, because who knows if I'm going to be able to.* Another opportunity came up, and I just didn't want to work for the same company for the rest of my life.

Yes, it can be difficult when our partner is in the Tunnel, and we're thinking, *How is this going to affect our relationship, our finances, or our family?* We may feel the tension rise up in our bodies. This is just our Human Normal survival instinct — it's OK, Ladies! We can soothe ourselves by taking three or four deep breaths and shifting into Human Spirit. Then, we can listen with openness and curiosity but without attachment to how it *might* affect us. Remember — it's not personal!

This is actually a good time to practice being a Queen — a sovereign, powerful leader of your own life, learning how to lead *alongside* your future King. Also, preparing yourself to receive is key because providing for the people in his realm is very important to a man in the King stage. I never thought I would have an issue with receiving, but now that I'm married to a King, I can tell you it was quite an adjustment!

Why Won't He Open Up to Me?

A common complaint from women about their men (in any stage) is that they don't share their thoughts and feelings. However, when we take into account the suggestion above to be more open and curious, our men will be much more likely to share with us.

When we come from a place of curiosity, it helps men feel safe to *open up* with us. They don't feel as if we are judging or criticizing them. A natural survival instinct for a man is to conceal himself when he doesn't feel safe, appreciated, or respected.

That's actually true for most of us — think about it. Can you recall a time when you felt judged or criticized by someone? Maybe it was a coworker, family member, or friend. How safe would *you* have felt to open up to them? Wouldn't that judgment cause you to conceal more than you reveal to them? When we instinctually conceal, we do so to protect ourselves, our jobs, the people we love, and our relationships.

I'll say this again and again: *to conceal is to protect.* It's not logic; it's instinct! Carter summed it up this way:

This actually may help me communicate some concepts with my wife because there's a bit of shame and some guilt, maybe because of the Tunnel experience. It's just very difficult for me to be intimate with her because of what I'm thinking about and what I'm going through right now. I never thought about that piece, intimacy-wise; I was thinking, "It's just timing." Or it's "You don't know me, you don't respect me." It's very difficult for me to be intimate with her because she doesn't see me in a positive light, which I find is a weird response even for me. Like, I should just get over it. But man, it's tough.

Can you see where he is closing up and concealing to protect himself? Sadly, this is very common in relationships when men feel criticized, judged, or not accepted for who they are. Masterclass 1-4 dives deeper into the concepts of concealing and revealing.

From what we have learned about this stage, the Tunnel is a very *internal* experience for men, which they often find hard to articulate. It is a time to really deepen our *listening* capacities.

This really needs to be said: Listening to a man is *very different* from how two women will listen and connect to one another. Women will often ask questions, excitedly interrupt and interject, and so on, which creates, *for us*, a connection! Our Diffuse Awareness allows us to hop between different questions, comments, and even topics without missing a beat.

For our men, however, this is not the case!

This is what deep listening looks like for a man: We ask him one question. (Not three! Just one.) Then, we put imaginary duct tape on our mouths and wait. Hear me out …

Most men are very *thoughtful* in their answers. They will take our questions seriously and often take time to think about what they're going to say. Our challenge is to be silent after asking just one question. Let him think about it and wait for his response. It can take up to two minutes! Talk about an uncomfortable silence for us. It's not uncomfortable for him; he's processing his thoughts internally. Most women in Gathering Mode process their thoughts externally by talking them out, right? This is another area where the opposite is true for men.

If we can be really patient, he will formulate his thoughts and then answer our question. When he stops or pauses, don't assume he's done! If we can just respond with "Mmm-hmm" or "Tell me more about that," he will keep going! What's the value of that for us? He will share from the depth you have been craving, and it will amaze you! You can then feel the delicious connection that most of us desire with our man.

> **How to listen to a man:**
>
> Ask him one question. (Not three! Just one.) Then, we put imaginary duct tape on our mouths and wait...
>
> Let him think about it and wait for his response. It can take up to two minutes!
>
> BARBARA COLE SALMERON

Men are rarely listened to in this way, and he *will* notice and appreciate it. In fact, when someone asks me for dating advice, this is the very thing I tell them. He will feel so heard and understood that he'll be much more likely to ask for another date! You will be amazed at how much a man will share when given the space and when he feels heard and respected.

Because men are very thoughtful with their answers and can take up to two minutes to respond, we tend to get nervous with that silence, and our Human Normal instinct flares up. Here's an example based on what countless women have told us in our research interviews about their internal experience with the silence:

Her: "How about we go out for pizza tonight?"

Him: (Thinking silently)

Her: (Thinking) *Did he not hear me? Should I ask again? Or maybe he doesn't want pizza?*

Her: "Or we could go get Chinese food instead?"

Him: (Shifting his *single-focus thinking* from pizza to Chinese food … The clock starts over!)

Her: (Thinking) *Maybe he doesn't want Chinese food either …*

Her: "Or you can pick a place for us to go. What are you in the mood for?"

Him: (Shifting his thinking from Chinese food to all of the other possibilities and experiencing frustration at this point!)

Her: (Inner cavewoman is triggered at this point, and she doesn't know what to think.)

Now, this is a very simple example of deciding on dinner, yet can you see how there would be even greater tension with a more serious subject? I invite you to test this out when speaking with the men in your life!

My experience in relating to and interviewing men over the years is this: I ask them just one question and give them silence and space to respond. The result? They can talk forever and share so much because they finally feel heard without judgment!

They even surprise themselves with how much they open up, often because of my guarantee of confidentiality and anonymity or because they feel relaxed when there is no right or wrong answer to my interview questions. This creates a sense of safety for them to share and open up.

That kind of non-judgmental space is huge for men, *especially* when it comes to confidentiality. If that space has been violated by someone, men will naturally start to conceal things from the violator rather than reveal them. This is also true for women in Hunting Mode, of course!

Be a Safe Space for Him, Yet Not IN HIS SPACE

Please remember this: *the Tunnel is only one person wide!* Regardless of our desire to support them, we are unable to be in the Tunnel *with* them. This is a journey that they need to go through *alone*. It is *their* initiation into the King stage — and we must honor that.

I know the desire to be in the Tunnel with our men, helping them work it all out, comes from a place of love and care — but please realize this is a solo expedition. We can still be a strong support for them from the outside, however. One simple yet powerful way to offer that support is to ask them how!

> The Tunnel is only one person wide! Regardless of our desire to support them, we are unable to be in the Tunnel *with* them.
>
> This is a journey that they need to go through alone. It is *their* initiation into the King stage — and we must honor that.
>
> BARBARA COLE SALMERON

Literally ask, "What support do you need from me right now? What does that look like for you?" Another fantastic question to ask, once he gives input about the support he needs, is "What would this support provide for you?" This is a deep question that he has likely never been asked before. However, it helps both of you because once you hear what your support will provide for him, you will *want* to provide that for him if you are able to.

In fact, this question is so good that you can use it in other circumstances with your men. Ask the men in your life what something (transition time, patience, respect, appreciation, and even sex) provides for them. Once you know *how meaningful* something is for this man, you may find you are much more *willing* to provide it!

By the way, this question works both ways! Right now, we are exploring what our men need, but you may be thinking *What about my needs? When do I get support?* I can tell you from personal experience that when we help others get what they need, they become much more willing to offer support and help to meet our needs. I've found this to be true in both business and personal relationships. So, become attuned to his needs, and don't be afraid to offer up your support first, Ladies! You'll reap wondrous and beautiful rewards in the long run.

The Stages of Development in Cookie Form — The Tunnel

I shared it right at the start of this section — men in this stage are in the oven, baking. Whatever cookie he has decided to be in the Late Prince stage is set, and being in the baking process, aka the Tunnel, is uncomfortable — it's darn hot in there. Soon, however, it'll all be worth it. He will be a fully baked King when he emerges from the Tunnel!

King

He's been through a difficult journey in the Tunnel, and now he has come out the other side as a King. This phase is delicious — it's where you get to enjoy the fully baked cookie. YUM!

So, after all that baking, what really matters to a man in the King stage? A King cares about *providing*. That is one of his main focuses, and he will often be asking himself (internally) "What am I providing?" as well as "Is what I am providing being *appreciated and valued?*"

Unlike a Prince, who's still discovering who they are and where they stand, the King's personal values are much more defined and strongly locked in. Tom, a man in his fifties who is about to retire, said this after learning about the King stage: "That must be where I'm at right now because that's the only kind of people I surround myself with now."

> A King cares about *providing*. That is one of his main focuses, and he will often be asking himself (internally)
>
> "What am I providing? Is what I am providing being *appreciated and valued?*"
>
> BARBARA COLE SALMERON

A Prince may still be quite open to feedback from loved ones about their life choices. He answers questions with more openness to different possibilities, as his values are still developing. You can add a little cinnamon and spice to that cookie dough!

However, with a King? That dough is cooked. We like to say that man is fully baked! There can be something deeply soothing about being in the presence of a man fully grounded in who he is. His core values are defined, and he's not afraid to share them. Carter, a man in his forties who relates to being in the Tunnel, shared, "Yeah, that resonates with me. When my wife asked me 'Why don't you want to do it anymore?' And I told her, 'Because

I'm tired of being that shitty guy,' or 'I don't want to be that guy anymore.' I want to align my inner with my outer. Yeah, I may use that because it's something that may help me to communicate where my brain has turned."

One issue that can arise here, however, is that there is almost no way to get him to agree to something that he simply doesn't want to do. He's got no problem saying "I'm not interested in that." That doesn't mean he is completely unyielding in his decisions. He still has a Worth-It Calculation that includes *you*.

Now, let's say that going to the ballet is not at the top of his core values (or even anywhere on his list), yet if you ask him to go with you, he may ask himself, "What will that provide *for her?*" and "What would make it worth it for me?" If he is aware of the happiness it will provide for you, it will more than likely pass his Worth-It Calculation! John, a King in his fifties, said it this way:

It's as important for men to take care of the women in our lives that we care about as it is for the care of the children. One of the things that would cause it to be worthwhile is to imagine there's an emotional payoff. Even subconsciously, maybe I get to pat myself on the back — there's an emotional paycheck. Oh yeah, what a great guy. I did the right thing. If it's a duty, then there's a payoff. You know, there's an upside. We get to feel good about living up to what we feel is our duty. Military service comes to mind. If you are fighting for something you believe in, then there's an upside. It's wanting to protect that which we care about.

A King's quest is now about aligning their internal values to be congruent with their outer life. In the stages before, he was still forming his personal values. As his values and ideas for his life shifted, so too did his actions. As a Prince, there was much more flexibility in how he maintained harmony in his life by simply staying in the process of changing, trying things on, letting things go, and trying again.

In my research, I had more than one man explain to me how he felt when stepping out of the Tunnel into the King stage. They would share what it was like stepping directly into clarity about their values. Their legacy, relationships, and actions are now all about getting lined up with who they have formed themselves to be. When I asked John what was important to him now that he was in the King stage, he said, "Integrity. If I've told somebody I'll do something, it doesn't matter how inconvenient it is or how little return there is."

When a King is in a job, relationship, or other situation that does not align with his values, he will experience discontent, angst, and discomfort until he makes some changes. We can see this happen when someone leaves the ideal "dream job" to follow their own passions and dreams, or because of a conflict of ethics. Once a King is clear on his values, he is *compelled* to come into alignment with them. I asked Tom, a married man in his fifties who is also in the King stage, what his top priorities are, and he said, "Making sure my family and my friends are protected. I'm that guy. I'm very politically active so I can make sure that people are doing what they're supposed to be doing. I have put myself in harm's way to protect people. I've done that on numerous occasions. And then, if somebody is down and out, making sure they get what they need to get support, to get back on their feet. I expect nothing in return."

> When a King is in a job, relationship, or other situation that does not align with his values, he will experience discontent, angst, and discomfort until he makes some changes...
>
> Once a King is clear on his values, he is *compelled* to come into alignment with them.
>
> BARBARA COLE SALMERON

In most cases, a man in the King stage will take into account his financial responsibilities before making a big leap, as the decision still has to pass his Worth-It Calculation! He will be cognizant of still needing to pay his bills and support his family if he has one. If he's unable to leave a successful job for another job or to start his own business because of finances or logistics, he will most likely stay. However, it will grind on him if there is a conflict between the company's values and his own. Jack, a married man and father of two, shared this about being a King: "For work, my 'job' is my goal to help as many small startup agriculture tech companies succeed. I just want to be one cog to help them do that. So that's the goal of my consultancy, to do what I can to advance technology through those companies."

I think most of us have experienced working somewhere where we are unhappy, and it's not fun! Being unhappy at work can take a big toll on a King's relationship with his partner and his kids, so he will continue to seek out a solution or resign himself to counting down the days to retirement. If this is happening with a King you know, you can listen and be a sounding board for him. You can help him solve the dilemma if he's open to that. The saying "Happy wife, happy life" also applies to the husband! It's easy to see how either parent's being unhappy will affect the whole family. This work is about turning relationship conflicts and misunderstandings into truly loving and respectful partner-ships. Jack shared more with me on what is most important to him now: "I also want to maintain the good family we have right now. I mean, there's nothing more important than that. It's just to maintain the tight family we have."

Important to Remember

Do you recall how we said that most men are always some part Knight? In my interview with Jack, I asked him, "What stage do you see yourself in?" He answered: "I'm feeling split between King and Knight. I think the King resonates with me because I think I'm past building as my primary focus and because at this point, I can afford to do more things on my own terms. Now, I also think Knight because I'm still doing and wanting to do a lot of new things. I'm adventurous professionally and also in doing new things in other areas, such as traveling."

Kings Will Share

You may have noticed this with the Kings in your life. Most Kings will freely share their opinions and advice. Yes — even when they're not asked! Think about what a King does for his loved ones: he is focused on how he can positively impact his realm. Part of that will be doing things for his realm, and another part is sharing information that he deems to be important for people to know and act upon (according to his values). Jack, a consultant in the King stage, shared this about his experience:

> Well, I probably always had those morals, I guess you could say, but part of the King stage is you have to be able to afford to. I mean there is some luxury in that, right? There is some luxury to being able to say "I'm going to teach this course" and "I'm not going to get paid for teaching this course because I have the flexibility." I tell people I wouldn't have been doing this consulting two years ago because two years ago, I was still at the end of the Prince stage.

A man in the King stage will share advice with others based on his experiences and opinions and can sometimes feel insulted if it is not followed.

Who does a King's realm include? His family, specifically his kids and significant other, and his coworkers, friends, and employees. A key question he will ask himself is, "How much of what I provide *is appreciated*, and how much of what I give *is being used* by the people in my realm?"

He will answer this question by how it is reflected back to him in his interactions. Are they putting into use what he's providing for them? How are people *showing* their appreciation? Mary, a young woman in college, sees this in her father. "I would say I view my dad in the King stage. I've always looked up to my dad, and he has shown me the model of what it means to be a professional and what it means to work hard. And he has obviously had to overcome a lot of difficulties, especially with his hospital trips and being laid off a few times."

If a person in a King's realm is not outwardly expressing appreciation toward the King, is not interested in what he's providing, or is unable to receive the things he wants to provide, the King won't want to hang around for very long!

Kevin, a retired man in a state we call Elder, had this to say about being in the King stage in the workplace:

In my last retail job, I had a boss who was a lot younger than me. When I first started working there, we were like oil and water because, of course, I was smarter than he was because of my age, and he resented my having some of those feelings. We finally had a blowup, and I think that the blowup kind of softened both of us because he finally understood that I didn't want his job. I was not a threat to him, but I did have some experience and some wisdom that I could share with him.

What Does a King Need?

As with all the stages, the King needs appreciation! He needs to feel appreciated for what he can do for others and how it is being received in a way that is in harmony with his core values. If not, he'll likely want to stop providing for someone who doesn't value his efforts. Remember the Worth-It Calculation in Chapter 3? *Shown appreciation* from the receiver can change everything! Don't we all want to be appreciated for what we provide to others? Rob, a business owner in the King stage, said this about shown appreciation: "Very simple words of appreciation on a regular basis or gratitude. The words of affirmation are very important to me as it makes me feel like I'm appreciated and the good things that I do for others are recognized."

Something to know about a King that is quite different from the previous stages is that around fifty years old, a man's testosterone is beginning to decline. This grants him much more access to his emotional center than he's had previously. It's important to keep this in mind about your loved ones. Things may seem to matter more to a King, or he may have a more emotional response than he would have had in the past. This is good news, right, Ladies? Now, you can strengthen your emotional bond with him through deeper conversations, more affection, and so on.

> As with all the stages, the King needs appreciation.
>
> He needs to feel appreciated for what he can do for others and how it is being received in a way that is in harmony with his core values.
>
> BARBARA COLE SALMERON

What a gift this is to a woman spending time with a King! Many women finally feel a level of connection with their King's emotions beyond what they felt before. The King stage can be a very sweet time to be savored by his significant other!

What other kinds of support do we need to give the Kings in our lives? If we're in a romantic relationship with one, the best way to empower our King is to shift into our Queen energy. To be able to receive what he's trying to provide for you is key to feeling deeply connected for both of you. Receiving with grace and gratitude is the crucial icing on the cake that will keep the providing coming!

Men in the King stage really do need to be received and valued. They need to know that they're appreciated, and they soak up this appreciation like a thirsty plant!

With regard to sex, Kings need to feel desired. Although their testosterone levels begin to decline, that doesn't mean they aren't still geared toward sex as a *biological need*, like most men. We provide so much for our partners in this area — it really fuels them. I interviewed a King who shared with me, "Sex with my wife is the rocket fuel I need to go out there and slay the dragons and provide for the family."

Rocket fuel! Isn't that awesome? If you are dating or in a relationship with a man, I invite you to speak with him and *ask him* what sex provides for him. Remember to be in Human Spirit and come from a place of curiosity and openness. This will help him feel more comfortable in sharing. Once you hear how important sex is for him, you may find yourself more willing to provide for this need! In my Masterclass 1–8, called *Orgasm vs. Intimacy*, we learn to discover how much is "enough" sex for you *and* your partner, as well as the roles that Hunting and Gathering Modes play in the bedroom! All of my masterclasses can be found at www.Grow.BarbaraColeSalmeron.com.

What a King at Work Needs

A King at work needs to get called upon for his expertise. They can get really upset if you're wasting resources such as their time, energy, or their connections. So, if you are in a workplace and you've got a man on your team who might be a King, don't start a meeting late! Start it right on time because he's going to be upset if he thinks you're wasting his time.

They also need us to be curious and respect their opinions. I interviewed Carter, a married dad who is retired from the military, and he said, "I'm no longer ignorant of how that cycle works. Feeling loved allows for respect, and respect allows expressions of love."

Ladies, this is *really* important to remember: **respect is to men what love is to women!** Most women deeply desire to feel loved, and our men need to feel respected! They've told us that when they are respected, they experience feeling loved.

Part of that is respecting their opinions because these are a strong reflection of their core values. These values are very personal to each man because he's used his life experiences, his time, and the places and the people that he respects to form his own personal values. He's used his entire lifetime to form these opinions. If you ask a King for his opinion and you don't take his advice, he will eventually stop giving you any advice at all. He views it instinctually as a waste of resources. Especially if he is still in Hunting Mode most of the time!

A King takes accountability for a thing when he gives opinions or advice. He feels somewhat responsible for seeing that thing through. A King can feel very disrespected if you ask for his advice and then don't act upon it. If you're going to ask for his advice, take it and use it because doing so communicates appreciation and respect. If you are unable to take and act upon the advice, at the very least, share how much you appreciate it, how deeply you've considered it, and why you're unable to act on it right now. This can help to *show* the appreciation or respect he's looking for.

The way that Kings show appreciation for the things that *we give them* is by taking them and using them. They may never come back and say thank you; however, if they take it and use it, it's their way of showing appreciation. So, remember to *show* appreciation to them for what they provide because it changes everything for their Worth-It Calculation.

I asked Rob, a fifty-five-year-old King, what appreciation provides for him, and he said, "I feel appreciated and recognized. It provides a sense of satisfaction and joy and happiness. It's the flowers of the garden that I put time and effort into to produce a healthy landscape."

The Worth-It Calculation for a King

As I shared above, the Worth-It Calculation for a King has to do with whether his internal values are aligned with his outer accomplishments and actions in life. There are things that he is compelled to provide and things that he's *never* going to provide.

It will, of course, vary from man to man. If you have a King in your life, in any type of relationship (not just romantic), ask him, "What are you interested in? Where do you spend your time, money, and energy?"

Kings are going to be very specific about this, and you can learn about their core values by listening and seeing where he spends his resources of time, money, and energy. It's a simple way to understand where he is at and what is worth it to him because he's only going to spend his resources on something that he deems worth it.

> The Worth-It Calculation for a King has to do with whether his internal values are aligned with his outer accomplishments and actions in life.
>
> There are things that he is compelled to provide and things that he's *never* going to provide.
>
> BARBARA COLE SALMERON

And again, many things will be considered worth doing when it comes to showing up for someone else if they are being shown *genuine* appreciation and respect for what their efforts are providing.

The Stages of Development in Cookie Form — King

So, if a King were a cookie, what kind of cookie would he be? He would be a fully formed, deliciously baked cookie. Kings will come in all different flavors. Quite frankly, some of them we will like and some we *won't* like! They are all individuals, of course, and what all Kings have in common is that they are fully, fully formed men, with their personal values all baked in!

The State of Elder

Elder: an influential member of a tribe or community, often a chief or ruler; a superior.

—Dictionary.com

We refer to this last concept of the Elder as a state rather than a stage, as not all men will become an Elder. From our decades of research, only about 12 percent of men will make it to the state of Elder. Most men remain in the King stage.

This state is characterized by someone who is *beyond ambition*; he's no longer driven to achieve and accomplish like he was in the previous stages. He is really focusing his senses on the privilege of life and feeling very blessed. The Elder is always talking about how blessed he is and how so many people have contributed to him. They are truly grateful for their experiences and relationships throughout their lifetime. They have the benefit of having obtained a long-term perspective on life. It's a joy to be

> The state of Elder is characterized by someone who is beyond ambition; he's no longer driven to achieve and accomplish like he was in the previous stages...
>
> The Elder is always talking about how blessed he is and how so many people have contributed to him.
>
> BARBARA COLE SALMERON

in their company! Kevin, a married gay man in the state of Elder, shared, "I talk to everybody I pass on the street, and I do mean everybody. And if they don't run away fast enough, I may even have a conversation with them! It's never about bad stuff. It's always about making them feel better." Kevin also shared, "That's why I have such passion right now for comedy. You know, I think that I have a little talent in there that I've ignored most of my life. I have found over the last ten years that a little bit of comedy for someone can be a little sunlight into people's dark lives."

An Elder has a lot of wisdom to share, and they won't push it on us, as a King can often do. When asked, they'll share their opinion, or they will often ask us questions to encourage us to take a path of self-discovery on our own. What's interesting is that they desire to minimize accountability during this phase, so they're not really going out and giving their advice if they aren't asked. Remember, when a King gives advice, he feels somewhat accountable for what happens when the advice is followed. But an Elder doesn't really want that level of accountability anymore, so they don't offer advice unless someone seeks it out from them. Mary had this to say when I asked her if she knew any Elders:

A law professor I know at Duke Law is seventy-two, and he is so accomplished in his career. Even from a young age, he was winning cases that he should not have been winning. He was going up against the most experienced lawyers in a certain discipline without even taking cases in that discipline before. And he was winning them in front of Supreme Court justices! And you know it's obvious that he possesses all this knowledge, but he will never show anything but humility.

I asked her more about his humility, and she said the following:

You have to go up to him physically and ask him questions in order for him to provide his insight, and you can tell that his knowledge is stored inside. He's not unwilling to share at all because if I ask, he will give me very good advice. But he doesn't think of himself as this distinguished, accomplished man who, just because he knows all this stuff, and he's done all this stuff, feels like he has the authority to give every single person in the room what he thinks about something, or what he thinks is the path to success.

Can you see how she just described a major difference between a King and an Elder?

In the Elder state, men are all about empowering others. The Elders might ask you questions to empower you rather than give out their opinion. This is the quiet guy in the corner, and it's easy to miss him because he's much quieter than the Kings! Jack considers his father an Elder, and he shared his reasoning: "Not just because he is ninety, but also because he's not going to volunteer a lot of stuff on his own because of the way he is. So, you have to approach him." When you do notice and engage with Elders, they will flourish and really come alive. You'll be surprised by what you can learn from the wise Elder!

In my interviews with Tom, a married man in his fifties, I asked whether he knew any men who had reached the state of Elder, and he said the following:

Absolutely, especially my grandfather and my dad. They didn't freely give advice — only when absolutely necessary. And when they spoke, people listened. My dad shifted to that probably about the time he retired. He was a mentor to a lot of people because he was really good at what he did. So, when he retired, that's when that shifted.

What Does an Elder Need?

If we happen to know an Elder in our lives, we might already get the sense that they need space. They're quieter and more reserved. They need us to ask them questions before they share.

Don't mistake their quietness for not having anything of value to share — they have a lot of experience and wisdom to offer. Support from us can look like listening deeply and making them feel comfortable to share from their unique perspective. So don't be shy to approach the quiet older guy in the corner because you can have a meaningful conversation with him if you just sit down and ask.

I asked Rob, a coaching client of mine in his mid-fifties, why he thinks his ninety-year-old father is an Elder, and he said, "Because he's not vocal. He doesn't speak his opinions. He doesn't pass on advice. He's quiet. He's been there and done that. He has no more goals at all to pursue. But if you ask his advice, he's happy to give it."

The Worth-It Calculation for an Elder

The questions an Elder asks himself are:

"Is this worth contributing to?" An Elder is going to be interested in providing on a much larger scale, as in for the community or for all of humanity. *If* he chooses to, that is. He'll want to solve

> **The Elder's Worth-It Calculation:**
>
> **"Is this worth contributing to?**
>
> **Is someone else better qualified to contribute to this?"**
>
> BARBARA COLE SALMERON

the big problems of the world. I'm working in partnership with one right now, in fact! He has assembled a team of medical professionals from all paths of healing and created a think-tank mastermind to solve the issue of Western medicine not being integrative nor collaborative with other modalities. He wants to solve this large-scale problem for the sake of the patients, not for his own personal or financial gains.

Most Elders will tackle such a project only if they have the specialized expertise or resources needed to solve the problem. They may ask themselves "Is someone else better qualified to contribute to this?" If someone else can do it, they're not going to spend their energy contributing to it. It's not worth it for them.

In my interview with Kevin, a sixty-eight-year-old gay Elder whom I met in a stand-up comedy class, he shared how much joy his new hobby of comedy gives him. Sharing that joy with others makes all his efforts in this area *worth it* for him.

I asked him what doing stand-up comedy *provides for him,* and he said, "Joy, just joy. I recently had a very unpleasant experience that involved family. My way of getting around that negative experience is by turning it into a stand-up routine. That takes the power away from it. I don't want anybody stepping on my bliss right now." The joy he receives is from bringing the joy of comedy to others. It's his form of contribution that he is willing to gladly share!

The Stages of Development in Cookie Form — Elder

So, What Kind of Cookie Would an Elder Be? He is a fortune cookie, of course, because he is packed full of unique and insightful wisdom!

About All the Stages

Now that we've explored the stages of development of men, I bet you're already thinking about all the men in your life (now and in the past) and categorizing them. That's normal. This is valuable information meant to *empower us* in our relationships with men. Can you see how understanding the motivations of each stage will help your relationships with men not only in romance but also at work and with family? Men are not just larger, stronger, hairier *women* who are misbehaving, just as women are not smaller, lovelier, more emotionally indulgent men! Yet we tend to expect a man to behave like a woman, and vice versa, and are confounded when they don't. I truly hope this book has helped you to see some of the invisible expectations we, as humans, tend to place on each other. Now we know why those expectations will usually backfire with the *opposite* sex!

Remember, please, please, please do not ever tell a man *his* stage! You're going to have an opinion after you read this book and feel compelled to tell the man in your life where he is at and why, and in many cases, he may disagree with you.

I don't recommend that you share your opinion with him about where you think he is at. If you want to talk about this material with a man and share what you are learning, then here's how you can create the most harmony in this exchange: tell him about the stages (or let him read the synopsis at the end of this chapter) or watch my Masterclass 2–1 and then ask him "Where do you see yourself?" You could say, "I'm learning about how to understand men and how to empower them, and I'd like to get your opinion on some of these things. For example, where do you most spend your time, money, and energy right now at this stage of your life?"

And then you're going to be listening for the following: Is he mostly about fun and adventure? Is he mostly about building, or is he more into providing for loved ones or giving back on a larger scale? Or is he in a place where he is questioning everything in an effort to find what's really most important to him? Doing this kind of research and having these conversations is a lot of fun and *so delicious* — as long as we lead with curiosity and open dialogue rather than by sharing where *we believe* the man is.

With all the men I've interviewed, they've really enjoyed these conversations and would talk my ear off for an hour or more! They were very thoughtful about their answers and appreciated the depths of thought they experienced during the interview. They discovered things about themselves and told me things they'd never told anyone, and I believe that was for three main reasons:

1. It was safe to talk to me because I was coming from a place of curiosity without judging them.

2. It was 100 percent confidential and anonymous.

3. They didn't have any history or baggage with me.

If the men have baggage with the person asking these questions, they might be a little more guarded and unsure about how much is safe to share because, let's face it, men are so often made out to be wrong, even when they've done nothing wrong. They too often feel they are "in trouble" with the women in their life.

If I'm teaching this material to a group of men, I'll ask something like "What does that illuminate for you about the men you have around you, now or in the past?" This question will open up things about

their fathers, brothers, friends, and so on. A man will sometimes have trouble knowing what stage *he himself* is in, so seeing the stages in *other* men can help him to discover his own stage. And some men will be torn between Knight and another stage because, remember, most men are always some part Knight! Most of them still crave adventure and new experiences.

What's in It for Her?

OK, Ladies, I know that when you first hear about these stages of men's development, it will seem very unfair and one-sided against women. I can assure you there is something beautiful here for you, too! By truly understanding our biological differences and the instinctual behaviors that naturally occur, we can stop making each other feel "wrong" for it! Or, at the very least, we have uncovered why men and women think and behave *so differently*, allowing us to release our invisible expectations of each other.

When we empower ourselves to empower the men in our lives, the floodgates of connection, love, and intimacy burst open for us! How great would it be to experience a relationship full of mutual respect, appreciation, and just the right amount of orgasms *for each of you?* This is entirely possible when we transform our relationship conflict into loving partnerships where everyone's needs are not only met but also exceeded. I know it's possible because I've done it. It was learning and applying this material that took me from a hot mess to happily ever after in my love life. I deeply, truly wish the same for you!

Tunnel, King, and Elder — Self-Reflection Questions

- What did these stages and states illuminate for you about the men in your life?
- Have you known, or do you know, any men who might be in the Tunnel?
- Have you known, or do you know, any men that might be in the King stage?
- Have you known, or do you know, any men that might be in the Elder state?
- What does this knowledge illuminate for you regarding your own life stages?

Stages of Development of Men

Page: Our little men, before puberty.

- What matters to them most: Adventures, testing themselves, and fun!
- Worth-It Calculation: "Is this fun? Is it a challenge? Can I do this?"
- Possible conflicts: Won't stick with something if it's not fun.
- Support needed: Freedom to challenge themselves with new things.

Knight: After puberty, growth and skill building, before settling on a career path.

- What matters most: Adventure! The pack (his friends). Testing himself with challenges. Practicing and improving skills for the future. The concept of honor.
- Worth-It Calculation: "What am I learning? What challenges will help me level up?"

- Possible conflicts: Telling him what to do or who to be friends with. He may not be ready to commit to a relationship or career path.
- Support needed: Freedom to explore and receive admiration for their efforts.

Early Prince: Looking for where and how he wants to build his kingdom.

- What matters most: Adventure. Exploring a career path by trying many things. Changing majors is common in college.
- Worth-It Calculation: "What is worth my time and effort? What am I interested in building? What stimulates my thinking?"
- Possible conflicts: Expecting him to commit before he's ready, whether in a career, a university degree, or relationships.
- Support needed: Freedom to fully explore themselves as they test and eliminate one path to try out another.

Middle Prince: Build, build, build. He is compelled by instinct to build his kingdom!

- What matters most: Building, seeing progress toward his goals, victories and accomplishments, and winning.
- Worth-It Calculation: "Does this job/degree/relationship contribute to what I'm building? Is this fun to build? Am I making progress?"
- Possible conflicts: Very little work-life balance. Can strain relationships.
- Support needed: Point out his wins and understand he is compelled to build. Give him validation and sex, and make the most of your limited time with him.

Late Prince: He's approaching the finish line with regard to his goals and has accomplished much.

- What matters most: Not getting distracted from reaching the finish line. Will start to make more time for fun, relationships, and family (if he has one).
- Worth-It Calculation: "Will this distract me from what I'm building? Does this contribute to my overall goal? Is this helping me with what I have already started building?"
- Possible conflicts: Focused on completing life goals rather than achieving work-life balance.
- Support needed: Validation, appreciation, practical support, and encouragement, such as affection, sex, and food.

The Tunnel: A time of intense questioning about what is most important in life.

- What matters most: Re-evaluating what is in alignment with his values and how he is spending his resources (money, energy, and time).
- Worth-It Calculation: "What *is* worth it? What do I *really* care about? What's *most* important in my life? Now what?"
- Possible conflicts: Can be viewed as a "midlife crisis" by society. He must go through the Tunnel alone.
- Support needed: Being patient, honoring the process, being there to listen, and being a sounding board for him. Be curious so he can open up to you.

King: A fully formed man who is clear on his values and focused on providing. Most men remain in this stage.

- What matters most: Providing, living in alignment with his values.

- Worth-It Calculation: "How much of what I provide *is appreciated*, and how much of what I give *is being used* by the people in my realm?"
- Possible conflicts: Discontent if not living his values. Needs his opinion respected and his advice acted upon.
- Support needed: Receive and value what he provides. Providing him with sex, appreciation, and respect helps him feel loved.

Elder: Beyond ambition and achievement, reducing his obligations to others. About 12 percent of men transition into this state.

- What matters most: Reducing accountability, feeling blessed, giving advice only when asked, empowering others by giving back.
- Worth-It Calculation: "Is this worth contributing to? Is someone else better qualified to contribute to this?"
- Possible conflicts: Quiet and reserved; he needs to be approached and asked for his wisdom before he shares it.
- Support needed: Space, listening, being asked to share.

Relationship Harmony Hacks Wrap-Up

Thank you for sticking with me through the end of the book! I imagine your brain is spinning as you ponder your next steps to creating amazing relationships and partnerships in your life. Anytime you need a refresher, simply revisit the self-reflection questions at the end of each chapter to find inner clarity and great conversation starters as you continue your quest to understand our fellow humans. Remember:

- What if there's a good reason for that behavior?
- What if no one is misbehaving?

I was once in a *very* difficult spot, similar to what you might be experiencing now. As I began learning about the real differences between men and women and discovering the communication tools that work best, I felt a bit overwhelmed and skeptical about the changes I would need to make. Would this new way of being really make a difference in my relationships with others, especially men? Implementing these tools and learnings has helped me to create a life beyond what I could have dreamed of, especially in my marriage! All the study and hard work were absolutely worth it, and I genuinely want you to experience big, beautiful results in your life, too. I've created a number of tools to help you get there, should you need them:

> Implementing these tools and learnings has helped me to create a life beyond what I could have dreamed of, especially in my marriage!
>
> I genuinely want you to experience big, beautiful results in your life too.
>
> BARBARA COLE SALMERON

- Masterclasses — I've recorded sixteen unique stand-alone video classes, which are 70–90 minutes each
- Videos on my social media and YouTube channels
- Public classes and events
- Private or group coaching options (when I am accepting new clients)

I highly recommend that you devour and implement the additional tools in my sixteen pre-recorded masterclasses, which are available at Grow.BarbaraColeSalmeron.com (look for Series 1: classes 1–8 and Series 2: classes 1–8). After that, if you want one-on-one attention, you can find links to my coaching packages and my contact information on my website, BarbaraColeSalmeron.com.

Let me be the first to welcome you to your new, loving, and fulfilling life filled with juicy and respectful partnerships and where all your needs are met and exceeded ... *You've got this!*

About the Author

Relationship Capital Consultant Barbara Cole Salmeron helps people decode the mysteries of the opposite sex so they can heal their relationship conflicts. After going from a hot mess to happily ever after, Barbara now uses her experience and expertise to decode human behavior to help others rock their relationships at home, at work, and in romance! Her clients call her their Relationship Shaman, as she provides multiple modalities during coaching sessions such as energy work, Emotion Code/Body Code releases, Shamanic chakra clearing, Archangel communication, cord-cutting, sound therapy, and more.

She is the creator of the Relationship Harmony Masterclass Series, helping others to END the battle of the sexes. Some of these concepts and teachings are penned in this and future books, serving her worldwide mission of teaching others to achieve peace in their partnerships.

As a certified and licensed expert in human empowerment, Barbara has helped thousands of people overcome turmoil in their relationships. Her teachings are based on over three decades of research interviews, as is her book, *Relationship Harmony Hacks*. As her social media following continues to grow, she regularly provides illuminating tips for all types of relationships!